Betrayed!

Stephen Harper's war on principled

conservatism

CONNIE J. FOURNIER

with contributions by

Mark J. Fournier

ISBN: 1515399400
ISBN-13: 978-1515399407

DEDICATION

To Barbara Kulaszka - a woman of courage, strength and principle.

CONTENTS

ACKNOWLEDGMENTS

My sincere thanks goes to all of the principled conservatives who have given of their time and talent and resources to make Free Dominion a place where the grassroots could have a voice. Thanks especially to those of you who contributed your thoughts freely and kept the discussion going. Many of the quotes and ideas in this book came from you!

I would also like to thank my husband Mark and our amazing families for their unfailing support through, not only the publication of this book, but through the years of stress, hardship and disruption that led up to it.

1. INTRODUCTION

A S co-founder of Free Dominion, an internet forum dedicated to principled conservatism, I have many experiences that I could — and probably should — write about.

Free Dominion was launched before the advent of the blogosphere, and long before there was anything in existence that resembled our current social media. The evolution of the media, its application to politics, and our many trials and tribulations as internet pioneers could fill several volumes.

Yet, it is those very trials and tribulations — FD's experiences of "disruption" as practised by a government that has now given itself the power to impose it on us all — that qualify me to warn my fellow Canadian conservatives of what our continued support of the Harper government may mean.

Now, with an election looming, I find that the thing that is weighing on me most heavily and begging to be put into words, is this, my plea to other conservatives to step up and defend our values from the very people we have worked so hard to elect.

I know that this book is not going to make me popular in some Conservative quarters. In fact I suspect that there will be people I have long considered friends who will feel hurt and betrayed by my words. For that I am deeply sorry.

But, there is no way around the fact that the Canadian conservative movement has lost its way. The same people who were motivated to infuse our country with the principles of freedom and democracy, and willing to stand on Parliament Hill to defend those values against the Liberals, have become obsessed with the politics of personality. They are willing to turn a blind eye to anything that Stephen Harper does, because keeping "our team" in power is now the most important thing in the world. Even if "our team" is now behaving worse than the dreaded Liberals.

There is no doubt that conservatives have an uphill battle in this country. When they are in power, there is no external force pushing the Conservative Party to remain conservative. Other political parties are left-leaning, so nobody in the House of Commons is going to be opposing moves by the Conservative government that run counter to the conservative principles of the grassroots.

We understood that when we founded Free Dominion. From the very beginning we said that the site would never be a "Conservative Party" site, but that it would stand for non-partisan, principled conservative values, and that it would hold right-wing politicians accountable.

Unfortunately, as the Conservative Party became more entrenched in Ottawa, and Stephen Harper consolidated all of the power by winning a majority, then silencing Members of Parliament and stacking the Senate, the grassroots members of the Conservative Party became less and less important, and less and less vocal.

In retrospect, it was almost inevitable that a ruling Conservative party willing to ignore and ostracize its base would begin to create laws that were obviously not conservative, in the principled sense. The Harper government began to completely disregard the most cherished rights of all Canadians, those of freedom of speech and personal privacy.

Instead of taking responsibility for what we have unleashed on our country, most conservatives have chosen to blindly dismiss the warnings of privacy and constitutional experts and stand behind their guy. American president Franklin Delano Roosevelt justified his support for a Central American dictator by saying "he might be a bastard, but he's our bastard". Current Canadian Conservatives appear to have taken FDR's rationalization to heart.

The last time we had a Conservative Prime Minister who went off the rails, the Party was split and remained so for many years. Brian Mulroney did a lot of things that infuriated the conservative base, and conservatives reacted strongly by withdrawing their support and voting, instead, for the new Reform Party.

This time there is no major alternative conservative party to attract the votes of conservatives who are disillusioned with Stephen Harper. And, I don't really think there is an appetite for creating another Party split even if there was. But, the fact remains that the misdeeds of Brian Mulroney pale in significance when compared to the gross attacks on our freedom that have been perpetrated by Stephen Harper and his Conservative government.

In this book, I will be making the case that conservative Canadians have a responsibility to keep our government in check. When a leader that we have elected goes off the rails and begins to dismantle the very fabric of our democracy, we have a duty to send our own people into the political wilderness until they learn to handle the unfettered power of a majority government with the care and respect it deserves.

Perhaps you are thinking right now that I am not giving Stephen Harper enough trust. You might think that he is not the type of man to abuse legislation that allows warrantless government access to our personal information, or legislation that allows judges, in secret trials, to give CSIS permission to do virtually anything but rape us or kill us.

His record tells a different story as I detail in Chapter ten.

But, even if you do trust Stephen Harper and discount my reading of events, he is not going to be the Prime Minister forever. You have a responsibility to ask yourself if you trust the level of power that Harper has consolidated in the PMO in the hands of every potential new government that this country ever elects.

If the answer to that question is "no", then we must accept that Stephen Harper, by ramming through some very perilous legislation -- most notably Bill C-51, the Anti-Terrorism Act -- has put future generations in danger. For that reason alone he must be stopped.

I will be talking in this book about Free Dominion's history and about some of our experiences with censorship and "disruption" that have occurred already, under the watch of our Conservative government. Unfortunately, there will be holes left in our story because, at this time of this writing, we are bound by an extremely broad court injunction that could literally land us in prison for contempt of court if we share certain details of our journey.

Despite this impediment, I will share what I can, and I hope I will give my fellow conservatives some important things to think about. What is our responsibility as party grassroots? As Canadians? Should we hold our own leaders accountable? If so, how?

All of these are critical questions that must be asked and answered by Canadian conservatives. We took the bull by the horns in 1993 and we showed the Conservative government of the day what kind of values we expected them to exhibit. Now it seems we have come full-circle and we are back at that same crossroads.

What do we do? Do we put on our blinders and satisfy ourselves with the fact that, after many years of work, "our team" is finally in the driver's seat? Or do we remember all of the things were fought for... indeed, all of the things that our forefathers fought and died for... and get back in the game?

I hope that by the time you finish reading this book, you will be ready to choose the latter.

Our chance to act is coming soon. Election day is October 19th, 2015. Let's make it count.

2. BEGINNINGS

THERE is a saying that is purported to be a Chinese curse, "May you live in interesting times, and may you come to the attention of powerful people."

Apparently this saying doesn't actually originate in China and nobody really knows for sure where it came from, but, in this day and age, one cannot help but appreciate the wisdom of the person who decided it was a "curse".

With the advent of the Internet, it is hard to imagine a time in our history that was more "interesting". The bulk of the acquired knowledge of civilization is accessible to any twelve-year-old with a connection to Google, and the power of ordinary citizens to express their political opinions and influence their governments is unprecedented. Political nobodies can go online and express their thoughts for the public to read, and they can even tweet their opinions directly to the people in power if they choose to do so.

Gone are the days when politicians could go to the media and proclaim with impunity that the public supports them on the issue of the day. The people are networked, and they will cross-check every fact that the media presents to them and then publish every possible counter-argument. No longer does the mainstream media have a monopoly on reporting the news and no longer do the people in power get a free ride just because they can get the traditional media to play ball.

As expected, this new paradigm literally brings previously unknown citizens to the attention of powerful people, and we are just beginning to see the fall-out.

This is a story of us, two very average people, a truck driver and a homeschooling mom, who used the new media to stand up for the things we believe in, and have paid a terrible price for it.

Our website has been almost completely shut down, possibly hobbled forever, and our future financial security has likely been destroyed beyond repair. In addition to that, we have had to endure vicious attacks on our reputations, and even had to worry about the physical safety of ourselves and our family. The common thread is that many of our attackers have had government connections.

Our nightmare started in a very innocuous way. It came in a thin white Priority Mail envelope. It was addressed to Free Dominion, and it contained a cryptic letter that referred to non-existent previous correspondence and invited us to make a settlement offer for some unnamed offense. The deadline for such an offer was the end of the business day on the very day we received it, and we received it around 8pm. On the top of the letter was the little logo of the sender. It was from the Canadian Human Rights Commission.

My husband Mark and I both knew at that point that our lives were about to change dramatically. What we didn't know is that the journey on which we were about to embark would immerse us in the sinister world of gang violence, government malfeasance, and legal warfare. And, that it would subject us to such a level of online stalking and intimidation that we would feel the need to, literally, go into hiding.

But our fight has resulted in some legal and legislative victories along the way, and the resulting bright light that was shone on the tactics of the enemies of freedom, at least for awhile, put some barriers in their way and slowed the runaway train that was created by Section 13 of the Canadian Human Rights Act.

In this book, we want to share how we, as ordinary citizens, attempted to use the Internet to fight for principles of conservatism and democracy, and how this fight would pit us against that very people that we trusted to lead us.

The visible fight that began with that letter from the Canadian Human Rights Commission was just the culmination of several years of challenging our own party to live by their own words, and it was just the beginning of a story we are currently legally prohibited from fully disclosing.

Sadly, we will also be making the case that the Conservative Party of Canada has so abandoned their core values that they have become a real danger to our democratic freedom, and that true conservatives have a responsibility to stop them.

Hopefully, we can inspire other Canadians to join our fight to protect our fundamental right to freedom of expression. If we lose that, we lose our ability to fight for anything.

Free Dominion History

Since the premise of this book is that the Conservative Party has lost its way, I think that it is important to provide some perspective on our own political ideology and how our mission has evolved over time as the political climate has changed.

You will see in the following brief history that, even from the start, our goal has been to work within the party structure to advance conservative values and keep our leadership accountable, and to give the grassroots a badly needed voice.

The result of this experiment has been most disheartening.

In December of 2000, a small group of Canadian posters on the American website Free Republic decided to form a Canadian chapter for conservative online activists. Inspired by the successful online campaign against the Florida recount in the 2000 election, and spurred on by a recent electoral defeat in Canada, Canadian Free Republic members (FReepers) began to organize.

The Canadian chapter began in a little corner of Free Republic, but it quickly grew to the point where stories of Canadian interest were threatening to overwhelm their board. We were encouraged by our friends on Free Republic to step out of the nest and to start our own site.

After some discussion, our fellow FReeper who went by the username NorthernRight declared that an appropriate name for this new site would be "Free Dominion". Everyone agreed, and we registered the name freedominion.ca. My husband Mark, posting as

"Entropy Squared", wrote the mission statement of the website in the form of an "About" page.

Our first problem was that, although we all had some HTML skills (you needed to know the basics to post on Free Republic or you could literally break a whole topic thread), none of us had the knowledge or skills required to set up a real, interactive forum. Fortunately, in our small group was a sixteen year old young man who called himself AntiKev. He had the technical ability and access to the software we needed, and he offered his help.

So, after much planning, on January 6th, 2001, Free Dominion was born.

Since AntiKev was a teenager with school responsibilities and a real life, we had to learn to manage the forum on our own pretty quickly. It was all through trial and error. We eventually learned how to upgrade to the latest forum software and, within months, created a new forum design with a black and gold colour theme and a new forum subtitle keyboarded by Mark, "The Voice of Principled Conservatism".

The subtitle was also our mission statement. The promotion of principled conservatism was the primary goal, above any party or any political figure. We were so excited to finally have a voice that it never even occurred to us that there might be those who didn't wish us to have one.

As you will see shortly, the attacks started before we were ever aware of them and we have been in defensive mode every since. No matter what the outcome for us, personally, we fully expect the powers-that-be to continue to attack online political activists (or, hacktivists, as our overlords like to call us) in every way imaginable, because politicians despise what they can't control.

Interesting times - powerful people. We hope that our story can be used as a case study on the tactics that our governments are using to suppress online freedom of expression. It may be too late to save our own skin, but if other people who love the Internet can learn from our experience and take steps reign in our government and to protect themselves we will feel we have done our part as cyber-citizens.

3. CANADIAN ALLIANCE DAYS

WHEN Free Dominion started in 2001, the Canadian Alliance was the dominant conservative political party in Canada and the old Progressive Conservative party was a mere shadow of its former self. Stockwell Day was the newly-minted leader of the Canadian Alliance and he had just tried and failed to win a federal election.

Many Free Dominion members felt that the old Progressive Conservative party abandoned their conservative principles in the Mulroney days, and they were confident that one more election would see the complete demise of the Progressive Conservatives and an end to the vote-splitting that had been keeping the Canadian Alliance from gaining power.

For the most part, the mood was optimistic and Free Dominion members were excited about the prospect of promoting the values of the Canadian Alliance, which was a mix of traditional conservatism with a healthy dose of Reform-style populism. The general consensus on Free Dominion was that a Canadian Alliance government would result in a government that was democratic and transparent, and that it would change Canada for the better of all its citizens.

We faced our first principle test in the summer of 2001 when a group of dissident Canadian Alliance MPs launched an undemocratic rebellion against Stockwell Day and split off from the party to form the "Democratic Representative Caucus" (DRC).

Free Dominion members blasted the hypocrisy of MPs who ran and won seats as members of a "grassroots" party engaging in "backroom politics" to oust their duly elected leader. One Free Dominion member said, "When the Reform started up it was composed of citizen-politicians, they have ended up as the epitome of professional politicians, thoroughly corrupted by the Parliament Hill culture."

When DRC MP Monte Solberg was interviewed by the National Post, he said, "I think it is quite possible for us to go back to the Alliance if there is a leader there who is firmly committed to mending the fences and aggressively pursuing a strategy to work together with the Conservatives." Many Free Dominion members saw this as an affront to democracy as the grassroots members of the Canadian Alliance had shown little interest in a merger with the Progressive Conservatives.

In a matter of a few short months after Free Dominion was born, members were already starting to use their online voices to hold their own politicians accountable. Of course, since Free Dominion was a conservative website, there was the expected criticism of the reigning Liberal party, but the site quickly became a platform to demand change within the Canadian Alliance party, too.

As events progressed, eventually, Preston Manning came out in support of the DRC and suggested that efforts to find common ground on social and constitutional policy should be put on the back burner in order to facilitate a merger between the Canadian Alliance and the Progressive Conservative parties.

Despite the fact that many Free Dominion members were former Reform Party members and, as such, had a high degree of respect for Preston Manning, we were utterly dismayed by his suggestion. Some said that he was throwing social conservatives under the bus, and one member bitterly described it as, "The abandonment of 'Principled Conservatism' for the sake of expediency".

The DRC members were soon dubbed "the DoRCs", (one member quipped that this was strictly for pronunciation purposes), and many heated discussions took place about the possibility of helping to get them unelected in their own ridings in the next election even if they rejoined the Canadian Alliance.

Stockwell Day eventually agreed to fight a leadership race and, as the Ottawa Citizen touted Stephen Harper as "the great right hope" with his leadership bid, Harper was very careful to say that he would have no truck or trade with "Joe Clark's Conservatives". Many were suspicious that that meant Stephen Harper would welcome back the dissident DRC MPs and attempt a party merger just as soon as Joe Clark was out of the picture. This, of course, turned out to be exactly what he did.

The leadership election and the aftermath was a tumultuous time. Social conservatives were very upset with comments made by Stephen Harper and his campaign manager Tom Flanagan that implied that social conservatives didn't have a legitimate role to play within the Canadian Alliance. In addition, several long-time Free Dominion members were convinced that Stephen Harper had stolen the leadership election from Stockwell Day.

They pointed to the fact that the ballot envelopes for the mail-in election were see-through, and that the ballots were mailed to a storage unit where they sat, unattended, for weeks before they were counted. They also observed that, particularly in Ontario, Stockwell Day had drawn many times the number of supporters to his leadership campaign events than did Stephen Harper, so the alleged Harper landslide in Ontario just didn't add up.

One of the first comments on the site after Stephen Harper was announced as winner was, "Something does not add up here.
Day sells 30,000 or so memberships ... Harper sells 16,000 ... Harper wins? Where did the math go wrong?"

Later, another member wrote the following, "124,162 members were eligible to vote. Of those eligible, some 88,228 or 71.06% completed ballots and got them in on time. Mr. Harper polled 48,561 ballots, 55.04% of ballots cast and 39.11% of eligible voters."

The numbers didn't add up, for sure. It didn't make sense that Stephen Harper would get three times the number of votes as new memberships sold, and that the very popular Stockwell Day would barely get the number of votes as new memberships that he sold. Social conservatives were already upset with Stephen Harper and Tom Flanagan for marginalizing them during the campaign, so discussion was extremely heated.

One member wrote, "I'm trying to remember if the envelopes for the National Council vote was the same special see-through envelope that was used for the leadership vote. Imagine my surprise when a friend picked up my mail-in-ballot, saw my leadership choice and said, 'I should throw this in the garbage right now.' "

But, despite the anger and suspicion, it was generally agreed that members should follow the lead of Stockwell Day who did not protest the vote and, in fact, threw his complete support behind Stephen Harper.

At the time I wrote:

> It doesn't really matter what we think of our leader. The constitution of the CA makes it clear that it is not the leader, but the members who are in control of the party.

> Now it is our responsibility to take that very seriously. The grassroots need to be mobilized to take back control of the party. That means standing behind Stephen 100% when he is representing us well and taking him to task when he is not. We hired him to do a job but our responsibility does not end there. Let's pick ourselves up, dust ourselves off, and get to work."

Free Dominion had stood firmly on principle when the leader of the party was under attack by dissident Members of Parliament who were acting contrary to the party constitution. That was an easy call to make. But, as we were soon to find out, it was a much more difficult task to hold a party leader accountable.

We were optimistic that it could be done, and we knew we had the right vehicle to do it, but we had no way of knowing just how determined our new leader would be to not only marginalize social conservatives, but also to dismantle the democratic nature of the party itself. This was just the beginning.

4. PRINCIPLES

UNFORTUNATELY, the leadership race was barely over when the new leader faced a principle test.

Ezra Levant had been nominated as the Canadian Alliance candidate in Calgary Southwest. By the time the leadership election was over, he said he had spent approximately $200,000 in securing the nomination and for the political advertising that he had already started. He said that he had doubled the number of Canadian Alliance members in the riding, ballooning the list from 1,000 to 2,000 members.

The problem now was that Stephen Harper needed a seat in the House of Commons and word in the media was that he had his eye on Calgary Southwest.

Ezra was a highly motivated young Jewish man who was passionate about conservatism and democracy. He was well-spoken, and he was a social conservative. He was obviously well-respected among the FD crowd.

Free Dominion members watched intently to see how the situation would play out. Would Stephen

Harper throw this young, democratically-chosen social conservative under the bus and take his nomination from him? Or, would he choose a more conciliatory route? Everyone knew that he had the power to take that seat, but he wouldn't do that ... would he?

On March 27, 2002, the afternoon before the beginning of Passover, Ezra Levant called a press conference. He said he wanted to set the record straight.

Ezra told the press that he and Stephen Harper had been friends for over ten years. He went on to say that the media had it wrong and that there was no issue between him and his new leader over the nomination in Calgary Southwest.

Ezra said:

In the Canadian Alliance, we don't make decisions in the same way the other parties do. We're democratic. We're grassroots. And when a CBC pundit gives us an order, we don't say "aye, aye!"

This is one of the reasons I support Stephen so strongly. As he said in his victory speech on Wednesday, quote, "I shall, as leader, always honour the grassroots democratic philosophy." That's one of the reasons why Stephen left the Tories. That's one of the reasons why Stephen is our leader today.

Ezra went on to state emphatically:

Yesterday, Stephen telephoned me and told me that, given the media speculation, we ought to conclude this question sooner than our meeting next week. And although he did indicate that Calgary Southwest was his first preference, he did not ask me to violate our party constitution, nor did he ask me to flout the wishes of the grassroots. I want to make that clear, to all of my friends and supporters, and to all of our party members who love our grassroots style: Stephen never pressed me to violate our way of doing business. He just didn't.

He talked about talking to Mr. Harper on the phone and he said, "The call was personal, and so I will not reveal the details of it. But I will say this, because I want to brag about our new leader: He says the exact same thing in private as he does in public. Do you know what that's called? It's called trustworthiness. And Stephen has it in spades."

Free Dominion members breathed a collective sigh of relief. Ezra said we could trust our new leader to honour our grassroots principles. Things were looking up.

Except, the very next day the Globe and Mail reported the following:

> Mr. Levant told CTV that he will step aside and let Mr. Harper run in the Calgary riding he had hoped to win. Previously he had said a sitting MP should resign.

> Earlier on Thursday MP John Reynolds, the party's interim leader in the House of Commons, said his office is pressuring Mr. Levant to set aside.

> "People in his riding are pretty upset with him. He made a commitment to the Alliance Party to

step aside," Mr. Reynolds said in a telephone interview from party headquarters in Calgary.

If Mr. Levant doesn't change his mind he may be ousted by his own riding association, Mr. Reynolds said.

He said several MPs offered to give up their seats Thursday, but party brass turned them down, saying the issue of Mr. Levant's seat is not closed.

The Free Dominion forum erupted in anger. How could Stephen Harper possibly take Ezra's seat when John Reynolds admitted that other sitting MPs had willingly offered to give him theirs? Free Dominion members said they were giving up their party memberships. It got so heated that Mark had to ask several posters to edit the profanity out of their posts.

Overall reviews of this decision were scathing, with the exception of one anonymous new member who stated, "If Harper had to violate a principle or two to get a seat in the Commons, so be it."

The general consensus seemed to be that, if this was his first principle test, Stephen Harper failed.

Despite the bumps, the forum grew at an astronomical rate. By April 2002, at the Edmonton Canadian Alliance Convention, so many people knew about Free Dominion that we were able to hold a banquet to celebrate Principled Conservatism.

Canadian Alliance MP Peter Goldring acted as Master of Ceremonies for the event, and it was attended by other Members of Parliament and members of the National Council of the Canadian Alliance, along with about 100 delegates. Even Stephen Harper, as the brand new leader of the Canadian Alliance, sent us a letter praising Free Dominion for its role in promoting and advancing conservatism in Canada. Mr. Harper's letter read as follows:

April 3, 2002

To Free Dominion Members

Congratulations on your Free Dominion Banquet.

As the leader of the Canadian Reform Conservative Alliance, I want to thank you for the volunteer work you are doing to promote principled conservatism. Thank you for providing a discussion forum for the Alliance's National Council Candidates. It is through hard working volunteers like yourself that we will defeat the Liberals.

The internet will continue to play an increasing role in the interactive citizen government e-relationship. Free Dominion is one of the many steps in that direction.

I'm sorry my wife Laureen and I are not able to attend your banquet this evening. I applaud your efforts in rewarding outstanding principled conservatives such as my good friend and colleague Peter Shuley. Peter's sudden death in November was a great blow to myself personally as well as the party. Peter's grassroots democratic legacy will live on as our party continues to reach out to average Canadians.

Sincerely,

Stephen Harper
Canadian Alliance Leader

That highly successful banquet would not have happened without the tireless efforts of Calgary journalist Janet L. (Jackson) Krayden.

Many Free Dominion members used the site to actively participate in the Edmonton Convention. A forum was created for the discussion of proposed policy and party constitutional amendments, and National Council candidate information was available in another forum.

Some of the National Council candidates actually provided their own material for posting on Free Dominion so that delegates could see where they stood on the important issues. We were proud of how we were using the Internet to facilitate grassroots democracy within the party in an unprecedented way. Many of the National Council candidates who campaigned on Free Dominion were actually elected. Not surprisingly, a large number of them were candidates that were opposed to a Canadian Alliance/Progressive Conservative merger. Those "grassroots" National Council candidates were handily elected and obtained executive positions on National Council.

For those who felt that Stephen Harper might be inclined to a "top-down" style of leadership, this seemed to be a reassuring balance of power.

Predictably, in this post-Convention era, several National Councilors stood against Stephen Harper's seeming intention to merge the Canadian Alliance with the old Progressive Conservative Party. George Richardson, Ralph Forte, Nancy Jahn and several others took a principled stand and paid a political price for it. They did this because most Canadian Alliance members were against such a merger, given that the old PC Party was on its last legs, and old "Reformers" had embraced a new kind of populist political ideology that was diametrically opposed to the top-down philosophy of the federal Progressive Conservatives.

Around this time it came to our attention that there was a conflict between the grassroots National Councilors and Stephen Harper. Mark wrote a scathing article on Free Dominion about Harper's plan to overthrow of the National Council president, George Richardson and replace him with his own "sock puppets" who would do his bidding.

With what turned out to be truly prophetic insight, Mark wrote the following:

> Stephen Harper's leadership of the Canadian Alliance is a cancer eating the party from within. Like the Liberals in Ottawa, he is making every effort to concentrate all party power within his office. There is much speculation why he would wish to do such a thing, but many members believe it is to set the stage to force a top-down merger (or some form of deal) with the federal Progressive Conservative Party.
>
> Whatever is motivating Stephen Harper to subvert the CA constitution and concentrate all meaningful party power into his own hands, it is killing the CA and driving away grassroots members in droves.
>
> It is our personal opinion that the Canadian Alliance may not survive the leadership of Stephen Harper, and if it does, what is left may not be worth saving.

This was our first real attempt at using Free Dominion to hold the Canadian Alliance leader accountable to the party grassroots. The Ezra Levant debacle happened so fast and unexpectedly that we hadn't had a chance to mount any opposition, but this time we had notice, and we knew we had to try.

Mark's article resulted in phone calls from friendly MPs and National Counselors urging him to tone it down, but the planned motion to remove George Richardson was canceled. We thought we had had flexed our grassroots political muscles against the party leader and won, so we were very happy. Unfortunately, the powers-that-be were determined to push ahead at any cost.

Less than a month later, the motion to remove George Richardson was brought and he was thrown out of his position.

When the news broke I wrote the following in a piece that compared the Canadian Alliance to a reality television show:

> A motion to remove the former president was moved by David Leskowski and seconded by Jerry Rice. Free Dominion's sources have confirmed that, in a vote of 25-4 with two abstentions, Principled Conservative Award winner, George Richardson was voted off the National Council island.

The removal of George Richardson was a violation of the party constitution, and Stephen Harper's involvement showed a blatant disregard for the separation of powers that was supposed to exist between the Leader and the National Council.

I wrote:

It is the responsibility of CA members to hold their elected officials accountable if we are to win the battle for the hearts and minds of Canadians. The Canadian Alliance claims to do politics differently. It was formed with the intention of placing power in the hands of the membership, and that is the reason it has grown to the point of becoming the Official Opposition.

Canadians are watching. They will be able to discern whether the CA is actually living up to their grassroots principles, or if they are only paying them lip service. If the Canadian Alliance wants to make inroads in the next election, it is vitally important that the members take ownership of their party by demanding that the leadership follow the constitution."

Shortly after I posted the article quoted above, an anonymous user signed up to call George Richardson a "parasite", and me a "pathetic schizoid". He left after being pressed to provide evidence that George Richardson talked to the press about party business, and he never came back.

Around this time, in June 2003, there was a move by the powers-that-be to complete some kind of merger, or at least a deal where ridings were split between the Canadian Alliance and the Progressive Conservative party. I wrote that, "The melodrama of the enduring courtship of the Canadian Alliance and Progressive Conservative parties is as titillating as an afternoon soap opera."

Even though the predominant feeling among grassroots Canadian Alliance members was that they didn't want such cooperation, we could tell that it was going to go ahead with or without our support. We were right.

Stephen Harper finally did get his merger with the Progressive Conservatives once Peter MacKay took over the reins of the Progressive Conservative party, but there was already a crack in the membership base with staunch Harper supporters on one side and many Free Dominion members (generally social conservatives) on the other. This crack widened when, at the first Conservative Party Convention in Montreal, I brought a motion to amend the party policy document to include opposition to partial birth abortion.

Although opinion was divided over this controversial amendment, it passed grassroots approval at the local level and at the regional level, so it moved on to the Convention. On Free Dominion the feeling was that, whether one approved of the actual amendment or not (and not everyone did), the ethos of the party demanded that grassroots-approved amendments should be considered at the Convention.

The one notable exception to that opinion was an anonymous user who signed up to tell me that if I brought the amendment I would be roughed up by the security guards that had been hired by Stephen Harper.

The night before the vote on that motion, Stephen Harper gave a speech where he informed the delegates that he would not touch the issue of abortion, but that he would make sure Parliament had a vote on same-sex marriage.

Many social conservatives decided to take his deal and vote for the same-sex marriage policy amendment and against partial birth abortion, so the partial birth abortion amendment was defeated by the slimmest of margins.

Unfortunately, social conservatives who made that decision were to be disappointed because Stephen Harper never did have a vote on that issue in the House of Commons. He only had a vote on whether or not the issue should be discussed. Of course, the majority of Parliamentarians chose to decline to go down that controversial road. It was an obvious "bait and switch", but it was too late. This was just one more instance of the "under-bussing" of social conservatives in the Conservative Party that continues to this day.

While these cracks were continuing to widen within conservative circles and they were being discussed on Free Dominion, the site came to the attention of Left Wing activists, too.

In an internet forum, a "troll" is a person who joins the conversation because they want to disrupt the board. They are not there to have honest conversation. Our first of literally dozens and dozens of trolls on Free Dominion was a character who called himself Yukon. He was really only interested in overwhelming the site with offensive posts and causing disagreements between members. Yukon was an eye-opener in many ways because our original idea had been that we could run Free Dominion without ever banning anyone. He showed us in no uncertain terms that if someone is only interested in vandalizing a site, there is really no option for a webmaster other than to ban them. We must have banned this guy 20-30 times!

Despite this, we always tried to run the site with the lightest hand possible. Banning was something we did rarely and reluctantly because we wanted to encourage discussion, not inhibit it.

Every once in awhile we would have a group of people come in and try to get arguments going on controversial issues, then others in their group would accuse the people who responded of racism or homophobia or some other "ism". These people would overwhelm the board with topics related to their subject of interest so that visitors to the site who looked at the most recent topics would get a skewed opinion of the purpose and philosophy of the board.

We learned to handle this by merging all of their topics into one, and allowing them to have the discussion if they confined it to that one spot. Since that took the fun out of filling the Recent Topics page with controversial threads, this usually resulted in the trolls just leaving.

Long-time members still laugh about "The Big Fat Racist Thread" that we started when a bunch of trolls filled the Active Topics page with racist posts. The argument went on for ages, but most real members didn't even look at it. Some of the discussion on that thread involved issues surrounding Israel. Two longtime Jewish members, EdS and Roy Wilson, were deeply involved in that conversation. They were able to provide a strong, knowledgeable pro-Israel perspective to counter the opinions of the trolls. EdS, in particular, encouraged us to allow the conversation to continue so that he could make his counter-points part of a permanent record.

Most of the initial members of Free Dominion had a strong desire to argue against unpopular ideas instead of suppressing them. Posters who espoused ideas that were opposed to principled conservatism were allowed to argue their positions as long as they did it in a way that was not deliberately inflammatory. This made for a very wide spectrum of opinion on the site, and some very interesting debates. These conversations, and our experiences in moderating them were key to the development of our personal philosophy regarding freedom of speech, which we grew to believe was far more important to the health of our democracy than any other individual political issue.

Although we have strong opinions on many political issues, we must, first and foremost, protect our right to debate those issues. If we lose that right, we lose everything.

In time, we were to learn that there was a more nefarious type of troll infiltrating the forum. They were not just trolling the forum for their own amusement, these people were organized on-line gang stalkers, and we had become their targets.

In fact, much later we learned that some of the most active "racists" in "The Big Fat Racist Thread" actually had government IP addresses.

Despite the harassment, Free Dominion was doing what we designed it to do. It was, at the time, the only means for conservatives across the country to meet like-minded individuals, to communicate, to distribute information, and to plan events and campaigns that were helping to promote conservatism in the real world. Suddenly, thousands of conservatives who had been essentially isolated from one another came into contact, and we were part of this revolution in political information systems.

While the Liberals were in power, our members planned rallies on Parliament Hill that often attracted hundreds or even thousands of people. Our first rally took place in November of 2002 and it was to support farmers who had been put in prison for selling their own wheat outside of the Canadian Wheat Board. The crowd wasn't that large, but we had a good turnout of Members of Parliament including Stockwell Day and Peter Goldring (who organized an information convoy about this issue from west to east at the same time).

Members of Free Dominion also organized a rally for America around the time that US troops went into Afghanistan. This rally drew thousands of people, many Members of Parliament, and Stephen Harper even spoke there.

Free Dominion members rallied against Bill C-250, Svend Robinson's bill that added "sexual orientation" to the list of protected groups under the hate propaganda section of the Criminal Code. This was our first foray into the issue of legislation regulating speech. During the debate leading up to that vote, a supporter of Free Dominion sponsored a full page ad in the National Post containing an article which explained our opposition to the bill. After that I had the opportunity to do a cable television debate with then MP Carolyn Parrish. Ms Parrish turned out to be very warm and kind. She even bailed me out when, for a few moments, my mind went completely blank.

I also did a radio debate against Svend Robinson himself. Mr. Robinson excused himself from the debate several minutes after it started, leaving the rest of the hour to me to answer audience questions. That radio interviewer called Free Dominion a "shadowy group", and many Free Dominion members jokingly and cheerfully adopted that designation for themselves because it was such a melodramatic description for a bunch of conservative Canadians who liked to chat about politics online.

Throughout these many adventures it is not surprising that many close relationships were formed through Free Dominion, and indeed throughout social media around the world.

Some Free Dominion members were housebound, but even the fully-abled had not been able to express themselves in the world in anything resembling this way. Real world meetings were inaccessible to many people due to distance and other obstacles, and the expression of opinion through television, radio or print media was strictly controlled by the publishers and producers, leaving ordinary Canadians without a voice. Before the advent of online discussion, politically-minded Canadians had to exchange information in person, and that left many of them out of the conversation completely.

The left-wing equivalent of Free Dominion at that time was a board called Rabble. That site was started by left-wing activist Judy Rebick. We had some "board wars", where Rabble members would come and troll Free Dominion and Free Dominion members would go over there and troll them, too. Eventually, I and Audra, the then lead moderator at Rabble, began to cooperate in keeping the peace between the boards. Eventually most posters decided to "agree to disagree" with posters on the opposing board and the raids diminished until all that was left was the odd rude, insulting comment.

During these early years, both Mark and I had opportunities to run for political office. I ran for the local nomination for the Canadian Alliance Party, and for the Conservative Party, while Mark was nominated as the

Freedom Party Candidate for Kingston and the Islands in a provincial election.

Each time we became involved politically, our opponents on the left began digging through our comments on Free Dominion to try to find something they could use to discredit us and the parties with which we were affiliated. Even though we both had tens of thousands of posts they could mine for material, they were never able to dig up anything particularly "radical" that either of us had said.

This has, I'm sure, been a source of intense frustration to our enemies. Rather than admitting the obvious, that we are just average Canadians with mainstream conservative views who provide a forum for political discussion, some resorted to clipping posts by other various posters, attributing their thoughts to us, and stating that we have outrageous beliefs, but we are just "careful".

It is not acceptable to the proponents of censorship that we, ourselves, say nothing shocking. They insist that, in order to remain safe from their attacks, we must also delete every comment that they consider to be politically incorrect. Since, from the very beginning, we have wanted to encourage debate about controversial issues – to oppose ideas we disagree with by presenting better ideas – this has put us squarely in the line of fire of the self-appointed cyber-censors.

The biggest offenders in this attempted character assassination were anonymous bloggers with ties to violent anti-racist groups. Their obsession with writing about us and posting personal information about Free Dominion members spooked us to the point where we moved our household to a different location and kept our new address a secret.

In spite of these precautions, a woman showed up at Mark's work one day, said she was his aunt, and began asking questions about Mark's possible assets. We never did find out who she was (he had no living aunts), or how she came to know where he was working.

This introduction to Free Dominion is to explain what kind of a site we have been running, and what we were doing that drew the fire of our political opponents. It is important for you, the reader, to understand what we are and what we are not.

A number of years ago, I did a phone interview with Don Butler of the Ottawa Citizen. He was very interested (it seemed) in determining what Free Dominion was all about. I went into great detail about my personal philosophy and the general philosophy of the site, but his article merely said that I "insisted" that Free Dominion was a mainstream conservative site. It was a step better than how he had described us in a previous article, but I was still annoyed that he seemed to suggest that he didn't really believe we were mainstream.

So, in response to that article, I compiled a post that contained a large number of comments by significant Canadians who had described Free Dominion, Mark and myself.

Below are an assortment of those quotes. As you read them, you should fully understand why we stood in shock as we looked at that letter back in June of 2007 ... the letter from the CHRC that accused us of promoting hatred.

"I am so glad Connie decided to accept this nomination to run as CA candidate in the next federal election. Connie is truly a national player in Canadian politics. She approaches situations with fairness, logic and enthusiasm. She has a passion for politics and works with diligence. Whether it is on policy amendments, campaign strategy or just plain protesting the (outgoing) Liberal government, it is a privilege to work with individuals the calibre of Connie [Fournier]."

– Siobhain Broekhoven., President, Canadian Alliance, Kingston and the Islands Constituency Association, April, 2003

"I have been impressed by [Connie Fournier's] tenacity and focus in doing her part in trying to help the conservative vision for Canada become a reality. But, above all, it is her motivation that impresses me...and that is her desire to have a better Canada, a stronger Canada, and a freer Canada for this generation and those to come."

– Ralph Forte, Former CA National Councilor for New Brunswick, April 2003

"That's what he (Dean Steacy) did to Free Dominion (which is not a "hate site" unless "hate" is now defined openly as anything Dean Steacy disagrees with): Steacy was registered under an alias on Free Dominion six months before any formal complaint was launched."

– Mark Steyn, March 26, 2008

"Anyone who spends ten minutes at Free Dominion understands that it's a website of more or less conventional conservative opinion well within the mainstream of right-of-center thought, while prone - as is every popular political site - to occasional moments of overheatedness in the comments section. That's it, that's all. There's nothing going on at Free Dominion to warrant legions of hack bureaucrats investigating it at public expense for a quarter of a decade, and counting."

– Mark Steyn, December 22, 2008

"I have no idea what Free Dominion was talking about on October 17th that caused Fawcett to send her e-mail. It was probably some election-oriented comment, about repealing section 13. Whatever it was, it was political – that's what Free Dominion is about."

– Ezra Levant, December 27, 2008

"Many of these individuals are without deep pockets -- such as Mark and Connie Fournier operating the online forum Free Dominion -- and while harassed by the HRCs have stepped into the breach defending free speech in Canada. The big shameful question remains where are the politicians?"

– Salim Mansur January 27, 2009

"I had better tread carefully today, for I am going to write disparagingly about an entire class of sentient beings -- and we should all know what has happened to Ezra Levant, Mark Steyn, Kathy Shaidle, Kate McMillan, Jonathan Kay, Fr. Alphonse de Valk, Mark and Connie Fournier, Marc Lemire, and a bewildering, quickly growing list of other Canadian writers hauled before the so-called "human rights" commissions, and shaken down with frivolous but financially ruinous sue-and-stall court litigation, on the suspicion that they may have entertained "hateful," politically incorrect thoughts."

– David Warren, May 18, 2008

"I'm not comfortable in the company of Marc Lemire, Ernst Zundel and Malcolm Ross, but I am comfortable in the company of Ezra Levant, Mark Steyn, Brian Rushfeldt and Connie Fournier. It remains important to make such distinctions."

- Ron Gray, Former leader Christian Heritage Party, March 1, 2008, National Post

"...four of Canada's most pro-Israel Gentile bloggers, Kathy Shaidle, Kate McMillan and Connie and Mark Fournier."

- Ezra Levant May 4, 2008

"Criticism of Prime Minister Stephen Harper has recently come into vogue on the right. Economists from the Fraser Institute have condemned aspects of Conservative tax policy. The Canadian Taxpayers Federation called the 2006 budget "Liberal Lite." And people associated with the Free Dominion Web site held an organizational meeting in May, 2007, to found a new version of the Reform Party. Are things really so bad that conservatives are ready to go back to the days of division on the right?"

- Tom Flanagan, National Post, Sept 2007

The 54 year old Fournier is co-founder of Canada's most influential political discussion forum, www.freedominion.ca. "Mr. Fournier is one of Canada's most hard-working advocates of lower taxes and a better a life", says McKeever. "I am honoured that he accepted my personal invitation to run as the Freedom Party candidate in Kingston and the Islands. He is a high-profiled example of principle in action which, I trust, others of principle will follow and support."

- Paul McKeever, Leader of the Freedom Party of Ontario, September 7, 2007

Mark Fournier, who operates a small-c conservative Web blog, wrote yesterday that the resolution to cut off debate on social issues "must be defeated."

– Gloria Galloway, Globe and Mail, March 9, 2005

Ms. [Connie Fournier] co-runs freedominion.ca, a Conservative-friendly Web site where the prayer meeting is being organized with the help of the anti-abortion group Campaign Life Coalition.

– Peter O'Neil, Canwest News, March 10, 2005

"While downtown streets were closed to pedestrians, school buses were cancelled in the name of security and protesters were kept out of the sight of George W. Bush, about 60 pro-Bush demonstrators were allowed to stand within metres of the U.S. president's motorcade as it left Ottawa Airport yesterday. Connie [Fournier], a member of a pro-United States website, www.FreeDominion.ca, and one of the organizers of the rally, said her group contacted RCMP when they heard Mr. Bush was coming. Ms. [Fournier] said the group alerted RCMP they intended to be on the parkway, just past the first bridge on the way out of the airport, and the force had no problem with them setting up a rally there.... Ms. [Fournier] and her group of about 60 was permitted to stand less than four metres from where the president passed. He smiled and waved back to the demonstrators as his car rolled past."

- Vito Pilieci, Ottawa Citizen, December 4, 2004

"There is a very good Canadian Web Site called Free Dominion, run by two people who I have met several times. Free Dominion is about Conservative politics and exchanges of thoughts and opinions. IT IS NOT OFFENSIVE!"

– Howard Galganov, July 25, 2007

While we expected to have some political enemies on the left because of our conservatism, it was clear that, from the perspective of influential people on the right, Free Dominion was doing what it was supposed to do, and, over the years, we had a lot of support.

In December of 2001, some people were pushing for cooperation between the old Progressive Conservative Party and the Canadian Alliance. The suggestion was that the two parties could have joint nominations so that only one conservative candidate would be running in each riding.

MP Peter Goldring started a campaign at that time called "Say No to Joe!". He said that there were too many differences in policy for there to be this kind of cooperation between the Canadian Alliance and the Progressive Conservatives. In his press release, he wrote the following:

> The breakthrough breath of fresh air was the Canadian Alliance/Reform Party's long-standing tradition of grassroots involvement in developing open and clearly enunciated rules and policies for our members and elected officials to be guided by. It is this cherished basic tenet of the values of bottom- up politics that we need to emphasize and encourage

today. The Canadian Alliance clearly defined policies and principles of the current membership must not be sacrificed for any reason. We must work together to send our principles and policies to Ottawa, not old-line, top-down politicians.

Many Free Dominion members agreed wholeheartedly with Mr. Goldring and were extremely grateful to him being willing to stand up for the principles that they held most dear.

Mark wrote a passionate explanation about why he believed our principles were of such high importance:

The Canadian Alliance is the only party in Canada that represents principled conservatives so the principles and policies of the CA are critical to the health of the party and to the hopes for the future of the country.

The principles of conservatism that define what the CA is, and what the majority of its individual members believe, are really all we have. Our principles both define us and provide us with our biggest selling point.

The fact that the Canadian Alliance has principles at all makes the CA a unique federal political party in Canada. Principles are one of the subjects liberals must always avoid because a quick evaluation of liberalism shows liberals to be without any real principles other than power seeking. Liberals also believe 'principles' need only be adhered to when they promote the political power of liberals but the same principles can be immediately discarded if upholding those principles in any way limits a liberal's grasp for power.

Principled conservatives can take pride in presenting their political viewpoint and we can cite words of wisdom, passed down through the ages in mankind's long march to liberty, in support of our arguments. We have a rich and honourable political heritage from which to draw forth our case.

Liberals, on the other hand, must conceal their political heritage and deny the savage history of their political philosophy. They have no great thinkers from the past to cite to support liberalism and the closer one looks at liberalism the more obvious it becomes that its heritage extends directly to Das Kapital.

Principles are everything to the Canadian Alliance. Without them we have no form or substance. Without them we would be no different than the Liberal/PC Party of Canada.

As we go on, we will discuss some of the issues conservatives have fought for (and against), and the principles that have motivated us to do it. We will also talk about recent legislation enacted by our Conservative government that we believe violates those very important principles, and we'll propose a way forward. We will examine two issues that were of great importance to Canadian conservatives - the long gun registry and Section 13 of the Canadian Human Rights Act.

There were very important principles upon which we based our opposition to those laws, and principles don't change. We will be looking at how the same principles call us to oppose Conservative legislation like lawful access and Bill C-51. If we do not fulfill our responsibility to oppose such legislation, then we are no better than the Liberal party we replaced.

If we do nothing. If we simply re-elect our current government after they passed such egregious legislation then we might as well change Mark's quote to the following and admit that we have become what we once abhorred.

Conservatives also believe 'principles' need only be adhered to when they promote the political power of Conservatives but the same principles can be immediately discarded if upholding those principles in any way limits a Conservative's grasp for power.

5. THE CHRC

UNTIL halfway through 2007, when we got that little Priority Mail envelope, we knew very little about the Canadian Human Rights Commission and its provincial counterparts, and we knew nothing of the monsters its enabling legislation had created.

I'm getting back to this story for two reasons. It was a crucial point in the history of Free Dominion so it will help the reader understand our perspective. But, most importantly, it is an excellent example of conservatives mounting principled, grassroots opposition to an unjust law, and it is critical that we examine those principles.

Like many other people, we had occasionally, over the years, heard about the mind-numbingly bizarre rulings human rights commissions (HRCs) would issue, and we had heard grumblings over a provincial HRC persecution of Rev. Stephen Boisson, but the CHRC and Section 13 were still just ominous clouds on our horizon. We perceived both to be political dangers, but we hadn't had the opportunity to observe in a close way the peril of what they were, and what they were doing.

It took quite a bit of time and perseverance for us to put the pieces together about what happened to us, and I don't think we can ever fully know the depth of deception and disruption that was unleashed against us beginning in the Spring of 2006.

We filed a simple privacy request with the Canadian Human Rights Tribunal in April, 2008 to fill in some of the blanks in our knowledge about our case. The process is supposed to be done in 30 days, but we hit hurdle after hurdle.

They just kept coming up with excuses why they couldn't give us what they had on Free Dominion. Finally, they told us that, since Free Dominion was owned by a corporation and not, technically, us, we would have to get a letter from the board of directors giving permission for them to release that information.

So, in November, about 5 months after we submitted our request, we headed for the CHRC office in Ottawa with that letter in hand. What transpired there was one of the most surreal experiences of my life! I wrote about it on Free Dominion as follows:

> Yesterday Mark and I drove all the way to Ottawa to take some paperwork to the CHRC. They have been stonewalling us since April on our Access to Information request for the files on Free Dominion and I had a document that I wanted to give them in person that would clear the way for them to fulfill our request.
>
> We got to the building on 344 Slater St. and took the elevator to the 8th floor.
>
> When we walked in, we did not encounter a receptionist like we expected. There was a

security guard behind glass, instead. When I wanted to hand him the letter with my case number on it, I had to slip it through a little slot in the glass.

He directed us to sit in two chairs across from his station and he disappeared into the back. He came back out in a couple of minutes and told us that he had given the letter to someone who would pass it along until they found someone who could "give us an answer". I thought that was rather strange since I had already said that I just wanted to talk to Heather Throop and give her a document.

As we were waiting, we heard a huge commotion in the outside hall, which had been utterly deserted. A guy came barreling down the hall with a cart loaded with files, grabbed an elevator, and disappeared. I turned to Mark and whispered, "There go our files".

A few moments later, a young, timid-looking girl came out and handed something to the security guard, whispered something to him, and then retreated quickly from our sight. I honestly thought the poor girl suspected we were wired with bombs!

The security guard then told us that Heather Throop wasn't in, but asked if we would like to talk to Deborah Cansick. I said that that would be fine because I have talked to her by email several times.

Mark and I stood waiting as the security guard walked out the back door of his booth and we prepared to go in to see Deborah Cansick.

To my utter astonishment, he, instead, picked up a phone in the waiting room, dialed a number, and handed it to me. I wasn't even allowed to see Deborah Cansick...I had to speak to her on a phone while she hid in another room!!

Well, to make a long story short, Cansick told me there was no point in giving her the paperwork I brought because they weren't planning on fulfilling my request.

I hung up the phone, took my letter back through the little hole in the window, and Mark and I left the office for the elevator. As we were waiting, an older woman and a guy with a bunch of earphones attached to him came and waited with us and got on the elevator as we rode down. I said to Mark later that it seemed like they appeared out of nowhere to make sure we actually left the building!

Both Mark and I were spooked by our experience at the CHRC. It was unlike any other government office we have ever seen. Talk about "faceless bureaucracy"! It is absolutely frightening that these people, who spend their days hidden behind a security guard and bulletproof glass, have the power to utterly destroy the lives of Canadians, and they don't even have to look their victims in the eyes.
George Orwell must be spinning in his grave."

One poster stated that he thought the behaviour of the CHRC staff was "delusional".

Mark replied by writing:

> That word came to my mind too. I can see a lot
> of people getting very angry with Canada's tax
> collectors at times, yet if you go into a Revenue
> Canada office you are greeted by a normal
> receptionist and can see normal office activities
> going on in the background, and can meet face
> to face with an actual human.
>
> The people at the CHRC must be delusional if
> they think they are in danger from the people
> they have been harassing and persecuting. I
> think it may also be part and parcel of the
> image the CHRC paints of Canadians-are-
> dangerous-bigots to try to justify their own
> existence. Orwell, Orwell and more Orwell.

Eventually we were able to get the documents from the CHRC and they were heavily redacted. Some pages were actually completely blacked out. We had to file an appeal with the Privacy Commissioner to get more information, and we eventually got that, too.

The documents that were reluctantly given to us by the CHRC helped us to fill in some holes, as has a review of the posts from the relevant time.

July 18, 2007 was the first day we became aware of the problem, but it began long before.

In the two years leading up to this time one of Free Dominion's most polarizing posters was an Alberta man, Bill Whatcott. Mr. Whatcott had three areas of political interest, abortion, homosexuality, and Islam, but the means by which he promoted his beliefs were often so outrageous that they eclipsed any message he wanted to convey.

He was prone to post graphic pictures of anything from aborted fetuses or anal warts to prolapsed rectums in the middle of other conversations, without warning. In an effort to keep the site family and work-friendly, we told him that he had to put warnings on any threads that contained such material. We felt that stuck a balance between his right to express his opinions and the desire of other posters to not be surprised by graphic content. Needless to say, though, he was also a very divisive force in the FD forum and his seeming inability to respect any social boundaries at all eventually resulted in him being banned - but not before leaving a CHRC mess behind for us.

We don't actually blame Whatcott for what happened to us because, we believe we were targets, and if the complaint hadn't been about something Bill Whatcott posted, they would have found something posted by someone else. It wasn't Bill Whatcott who the CHRC wanted to bring down, it was Free Dominion, and the two of us, who they already had in their crosshairs.

Although we had no reason to notice it at the time, the targeting of Free Dominion had officially begun over a year earlier on April 5, 2006 with the registration of a new member at Free Dominion using the pseudonym "jadewarr". Incidentally, this was just less than two months after Stephen Harper was sworn in as Canada's new Prime Minister on February 6, 2006.

We would not learn the significance of the "jadewarr" registration until May 25, 2008. On that date we were part of a large audience who sat in on the cross-examination of CHRC employees in the Lemire hearings held in Ottawa by the Canadian Human Rights Tribunal. In front of the tribunal and media observers including Mark Steyn, the CHRC was forced to admit that the jadewarr internet pseudonym was in fact an ID that was used by the CHRC's thought crimes unit while investigating complaints against websites. The testimony by CHRC investigator Dean Steacy revealed that several CHRC employees had access to the jadewarr email address, ID and password.

When written testimony from Dean Steacy confirmed that he used the "jadewarr" id in his investigations we immediately did a search of Free Dominion's membership list and found his user profile.

Mark wrote a piece entitled, "CHRC operative Dean Steacy is a Free Dominioner". Below is part of what that piece contained:

"Part of [Dean Steacy's written] testimony is reproduced here:

1. Do any investigators post on Stormfront.org?

I am not aware of any investigator other than me, who has posted on Stormfront.

2. Getting back to Jadewarr, do Commission employees sign up accounts on Stormfront, under pseudonyms such as "Jadewarr"?

I used the Jadewarr email address to create an account on Stormfront. I am not aware whether or not other investigators have created other accounts on Stormfront.

3. Do you know who Jadewarr is?

Jadewarr is not a person, it is an email address and a user account on Stormfront.org. I created *the Jadewarr email address on yahoo.ca and the Jadewarr account on Stormfront. I have used the Jadewarr email address and the Jadewarr account on Stormfront on occasion, **in the course of investigating complaints.** I am not aware of anyone else having used the Jadewarr email address or account.*

4. To your knowledge, is Jadewarr a Commission employee?

See above.

5. As part of your duties, have you ever signed up with a message board and made postings?

Yes, I have done so using the Jadewarr account in investigating section 13 complaints.

One of the many questions remaining to be answered is why did CHRC operative Dean Steacy register at Free Dominion using his official Section 13 complaint screen name 'jadewarr' on April 5, 2006?

Note he used the same official investigative email address jadewarr@yahoo.ca he spoke of in his testimony.

The date of the CHRC's jadewarr registration at Free Dominion is significant because it came before any complaint was filed against Free Dominion. In the oral hearing, CHRC investigator Dean Steacy refused to explain why he had started investigating Free Dominion prior to a complaint being made so we have no evidence as to who directed his attention to our website. All we know is that, out of the blue, a government agent had been assigned by someone to watch our site.

About three weeks after the FD registration of jadewarr, Bill Whatcott gave Dean Steacy something to watch. He began another of his political activism campaigns by handing out leaflets at the University of Saskatchewan. These leaflets were typical of Whatcott's style. They contained pictures including the famous cartoon of Mohammad with a bomb on his head that had sparked Islamic violence worldwide, and a very graphic picture of a school girl who had been beheaded by Muslim extremists. Below the pictures was text questioning why homosexuals were so supportive of Islam while homosexuals were being executed in Islamic countries solely for their sexual orientation. At the bottom of the tract he said if readers wanted more information they should go to the thread he had started at Free Dominion.

Bill Whatcott had indeed started a thread about his leafleting campaign at Free Dominion giving the time and location of where he would be handing out his leaflets. Included on his thread was a link to another website where Whatcott had uploaded a copy of his leaflet. With the link he posted at FD he also added a graphic content warning to anyone considering clicking on his link.

Allegedly, one of the people Bill Whatcott handed a flyer to on that spring day in Saskatchewan was Marie-Line Gentes. Ms. Gentes was, apparently, offended on behalf of Muslims (a group to which she does not belong) and filed a CHRC complaint against Whatcott with the Canadian Human Rights Commission.

Mark expressed our confusion and suspicion over the Free Dominion investigation in the piece he wrote about Dean Steacy's FD jadewarr account:

According to the documents Connie and I were served from the Canadian Human Rights Commission last summer, Marie-Line Gentes did not bring Free Dominion to the commission's attention with her bogus complaint against us until September 29th, 2006, over five months after Dean Steacy began his 'investigation' by registering as jadewarr. It may be coincidence, but the posting that ultimately caused poor Ms. Gentes such distress happened to be posted just two weeks after Dean Steacy began his complaintless investigation of Free Dominion by registering.

Why was Dean Steacy investigating Free Dominion half a year before any complaint was filed? And is there a connection between Dean Steacy and Marie-Line Gentes?

After our long and hard-fought Freedom of Information battle we were able to glean some of how the case evolved from a complaint against Bill Whatcott into a case against the two of us and against Free Dominion.

We have seen no evidence that at the time of the filing of the Gentes complaint against Whatcott that she had any interest in Free Dominion whatsoever. It appears she had never been to our website, knew nothing about it, and held no opinion at all about the site. We had never hit her radar screen.

Her beef was with Bill Whatcott, and him only, as she made clear in her complaint. This presented a problem for the CHRC. The CHRC rightly decided that Gentes' complaint against Whatcott fell outside of their jurisdiction, it was a matter she should have taken to the provincial human rights commission of Saskatchewan, the province where the leafleting campaign took place.

But the tenuous connection to Free Dominion seemed to be too tempting for the CHRC to pass up. They convinced Ms Gentes to change the target of her complaint to the two of us and to Free Dominion. They coldly used her for their own purposes.

The documents we managed to wring out of the CHRC's files also gave insights into the insulated atmosphere and culture of the CHRC's thought crimes unit. No less than 14 CHRC bureaucrats and lawyers were investigating Free Dominion and emailing each other about us. Free Dominion was repeatedly referred to as a hate site by CHRC investigators and their bosses in their internal communications.

According to the CHRC's documents they had another complaint against Free Dominion that they did not act on, which is now dead because Section 13.1 of the Canadian Human Rights Act has been repealed.

There was also a letter that was written to the commission regarding the two of us and our website. That letter was the completely blacked-out document referred to earlier. The reason they gave for refusing to let us see any part of this letter was that we would immediately be able to deduce its author from its content and they did not want to reveal the author.

We have speculated that the author of the mysterious letter might be the same person who filed the second complaint against us and possibly the person who also directed Dean Steacy to begin his official investigation of Free Dominion prior to a complaint ever being made against the site, but it is highly unlikely that we will ever find that out.

Regarding the complainant, Marie-Line Gentes, to this day we know nothing about her. She represents a hole in our knowledge of these events and we don't know if that part of the story will ever be told. Of course we wondered if she was somehow, even tangentially, associated with the hate propaganda unit, but in light of what we learned from the disclosed CHRC documents, we are now inclined to accept her as she originally represented herself. To the CHRC she was just a serendipitous pawn.

The Complaint

July 18, 2007 was a busy day for us. Free Dominion was hitting its stride, Bill Whatcott was testing the last limits of our patience, and our wedding was only eleven days away. It was early evening before we got home and had time to look at our mail. We weren't expecting the overnight delivery letter from the CHRC and when we read its content we thought we were being pranked. The letter basically said we were the subject of a Canadian Human Rights Commission investigation and, although they hadn't deigned to enclose a copy of the complaint against us, we had until the close of business on July 18, 2007 to file our complete response ... a deadline that had passed about an hour earlier.

Whether the letter from the CHRC was real or a spoof, and we suspected the latter, we knew we had a story and we immediately broke it live on Free Dominion. The thread "Human Rights attack on Free Dominion" ultimately generated close to 1,500 replies and nearly a quarter million page views. This thread was the second pebble of an avalanche, the first had dropped a day earlier at the CHRC offices in Ottawa.

The day before that, July 16, 2007, and two days before our first notification of the complaint (and our missed deadline to respond) Marie-Line Gentes contacted the CHRC by telephone to tell them she had changed her mind and wanted to drop the complaint. This could have, and should have, ended the affair, particularly because at that point we still knew nothing about it. But someone at the CHRC just couldn't let it go.

Inexplicably, the next day after the withdrawal request, someone ordered that the letter we finally received be generated and in our hands by the following day. Those orders were followed. Things would be so different today had that first pebble never been dropped.

After receiving the complaint, Mark posted the following in the forum:

> We have been waiting for six and a half years and the day has finally arrived, somebody is going to try to silence Free Dominion using the Canadian Human Rights Commission.
>
> Moments ago we found this in Free Dominion's mailbox:
>
> July 16, 2007
>
> File 2006057
>
> Dear Ms. [Fournier]:
>
> I am the investigator designated under Part III of the *Canadian Human Rights Act* to investigate the complaint of Ms. [name omitted at this time] against Free Dominion. As the investigator, it is my responsibility to gather the evidence in relation to the complainant's allegations and, once the investigation is

complete, to report on my findings to the Members of the Commission.

The report will include a recommendation for the disposition of the complaint. I can recommend that a conciliator be appointed, if the evidence supports the allegations in the complaint, or that the complaint be dismissed, if the allegations are not supported by the evidence. I can also recommend to the Commission that a settlement be approved if the parties reach an agreement during the course of the investigation.

I am currently awaiting your full response to the allegations which is due on 18 July 2007.

I would like to draw your attention to section 48 of the *Canadian Human Rights Act* which allows the parties to settle a complaint in the course of investigation. I would be pleased to discuss the possibility of a settlement with you or your representative at any time.

You can reach me at the address and telephone number indicated at the bottom of the first page of this letter. My direct line is 999-999-9999 and my email address is OfficersName@chrc-ccdp.ca. Please note that there are security and confidentiality risks in sending information by email.

Yours Sincerely,

Officer's Name
Investigator

This looks real. It appears to be written on official Canadian Human Rights Commission letterhead stationery.

Other than the last name of the complainant, this doesn't tell us much. It doesn't say what the complaint is about or anything else. Notice also that Connie was supposed to have responded to it by July 18, 2007, which is today. It was a fluke that we even checked the mailbox before we came home.

Somebody has likely decided that because they can't defeat some argument presented by someone at Free Dominion they will instead try to silence the whole site. It isn't going to work.

We will be keeping everybody posted on each development as it occurs. If this persecution actually proceeds it will not be under the cover of darkness, we will keep a very bright light shining every step of the way.

I promise.

He deliberately omitted the names and contact information of the complainant and the CHRC staff because we were working under the assumption that this had to be a hoax. Free Dominion regulars started to reply on the thread and most of them had the same opinion. The fact it was a letter mailed the day before, that didn't require a signature, and that we had been given no details and an impossible deadline just didn't add up to most of the forum participants.

We had a good long time to speculate about it because the office was closed so we had to wait until the next day to call and find out what was going on. In the meantime we were able to confirm that the phone contact information, indeed led to the voicemail of the CHRC investigator who signed the letter and that the mailing address and other details checked out. As the hours went by we started to consider what it would mean to us and to Free Dominion if this was real.

One poster gave voice to our unspoken fear when he wrote:

> At risk of ratcheting up the paranoia, I wonder if a kangaroo court case against FD might be politically motivated. Specifically, I wonder if it may have been launched, not by our standard foes the Libranos, Dippers, Blocheads and their ilk, but by someone within the CPC. After all, there has been considerable criticism of Harper and company's hard left turns lately. I don't think it unimaginable that someone involved with the Conservative Party might take a dim view of criticism on FD, and use Canada's collectivist machinery to silence criticism.

Our criticism had certainly been increasingly as we struggled to hold our party leadership accountable. But, would they use their government bureaucrats to take down a conservative message board?

Mark made regular appearances on the thread as I was in the background doing fact-checking in those early hours. He summed up our position very well when he said:

> I will not abide by an order to remain silent. If the CHRC is going to attack us they aren't going to have my help giving them the cover of darkness or silence.

intend to use this case to give Canadians a grand tour of the workings of the Canadian Human Rights Commission. This one is going to happen in a glaring light.

We didn't know much about Human Rights Commissions, but we knew instinctively that if we didn't make this as public as possible, we were going to be destroyed.

Several people started talking right away about starting a fundraiser for our legal defence. We were touched by their thoughtfulness and their willingness to stand behind us. We were not alone. One of the more heartwarming posts came from a young man who said that he didn't have money to contribute but he knew we should have a good notebook in order to keep notes about the case as it progressed. He said he had one, posted a picture, and promised to mail it the next day.

The next morning we were finally able to get in touch with the CHRC office. It was incredibly frustrating because, despite talking to two separate people who were obviously at computers with our case open in front of them, they refused to give us even a hint as to what all of this was about.

Many hours later we were given the name of the complainant and the link to the thread that was the subject of the complaint. To pass the time, forum members had created and voted in a poll guessing which poster would be the subject of the complaint. 51% of them correctly guessed it would be Bill Whatcott.

When we looked at the thread we were struck by the fact that the pictures, which seemed to be what caused Ms Gentes the most distress, were not even visible on our site. There was a link at the beginning of the thread and it was clearly marked saying that it led to graphic material.

The text of his flyer, which was essentially a theological debate over Christianity vs Islam, was reproduced on our site, and she did take issue with a couple of sentences contained in those paragraphs.

She also quoted in her complaint four other pretty innocuous sentences, but did not give links to their location so it took us awhile to find them. We eventually found three of those four quotes (to this day we have not found the fourth), and we found that all of them were connected to two anonymous posters that we later discovered had posted from government IP addresses.

Were those comments planted there to beef up a potential complaint? We don't know and I'm sure we never will. But, I will say that they stood out.

Bill Whatcott took a virtual beating on that thread from other posters who had little patience for his over-the-top tactics. It was amazing that the CHRC could find anything on that thread that was even an expression of agreement with his message, but, thanks to our government buddies, the CHRC had a little something to work with.

I say "a little" because below are the exact words that were the subject of the complaint. The first three are by Bill Whatcott:

- 03/09/06 "To see the original hitting Edmonton mailboxes tonight. (warning disturbing but necessary photo) http://takebackcanada.com/whatcott.html "

- 04/24/06 "I can't figure out why the homosexuals I ran into are on the side of the Muslims. After all, Muslims who practice Sharia law tend to advocate beheading homosexuals."

- 03/09/06 "I defy Islamic censorship and speak about what I believe is the truth about violent Islamism and its threat to religious liberty in Canada."

The next two are by posters with government ties:

- "How many of us pay nothing but lip service to the Muslim threat here in Canada?"

- "I have to ask why we are importing them here?"

The third comment, in context, is an obviously sarcastic response to one of the government guys:

- "Probably everyone want to jail a Muslim."

And the last one has never been found on Free Dominion:

- "Islamic fundamentalism and its threat to Canada's religious and civil liberties."

As you can see, the comments were quite typical of Internet political debate. Even by themselves, it is hard to see how they could have been found to reach the level of "hate propaganda", but they were written on a thread where they are roundly debunked by other posters.

The fact that a couple of them were written by people with government IP addresses is more than a little disturbing.

Interestingly, while we were waiting for word on the contents of the complaint another poster decided to give us an illustration of what kind of material was considered to be hateful under Section 13.1 of the Canadian Human Rights Act. The poster referenced a racist song that formed part of a complaint against a person named Glenn Bahr, and he posted that song on Free Dominion.

It was not until I was doing research for this book that I noticed he had done that. It was in the middle of a thread that accumulated 1,500 posts in about 4 days. But, the interesting thing about that poster is that, according to his LinkedIn page, he worked for both the Department of National Defence and the Vancouver Police Department.

Was he working in concert with the government guys who posted on the original thread? Was he deliberately posting something that had already been found to be hateful on Free Dominion so that the CHRC could later use it to beef up their case against us? I'm glad we didn't have to find out.

As members waited for news, they had time to reflect on our conservative beliefs and how they applied to situations like this. Some got very philosophical. I quote two of them here so that you can see that, from the very beginning, we were trying to look at the situation from a principled standpoint, and the conclusions we reached in July of 2007 are every bit as relevant and important today.

One poster wrote:

...if the complainant is really concerned about putting down racism, rather than filing an unjustified and unwarranted complaint against Connie, she should be thanking her for allowing these views to be debated and defeated on FD... In places like FD, everything is on the board for discussion. Good positions survive and change people's perspectives. Bad positions are marginalized and booted.

Racism can never survive in an open society where it can be confronted. But it can percolate under the surface for years until one day, it rears its ugly head and causes a lot more damage than otherwise would have been possible.

So, the first principle was that the answer to hate speech is more speech.

Another poster wrote an explanation of the process and commented on the fact that the complainant did not need to hire a lawyer. He said:

My understanding of it is that the Commission is added as a party - one of the plaintiffs - and the Commission has its own lawyers. The complainant can get their own if they like, but why bother? They can let the government do their dirty work for them.

Later the same poster went on to say:

The HRC lawyer is running a parallel case and they can just go along for the ride. That's what makes the whole process smack of a criminal prosecution, but without the procedural protections and a burden of proof on the state beyond a reasonable doubt.

So, the second principle that we agreed was being violated was the right to due process.

Another poster summed up our early feelings very well when she wrote:

This is actually scarier then I originally thought it would be. A person can put people through this mess both emotionally and financially, (you already need lawyers) because she feels discriminated against by a comment that has no association with her person in any way shape or form. Is this for real? Unbelievable. I am truly stunned.

We were, indeed, truly stunned. But, we would have been even more stunned had we known that summer of 2007 that eight years later ... a time period that saw our school-aged children leave the nest, three of them get married and three grandchildren added to our lives...we would still be dealing with the fallout of that little   white   envelope.

6. CHRC AND OUR PRINCIPLES

THE Gentes complaint against Free Dominion and myself was, of course, dropped. We found out on August 3, of 2007 that Marie-Line Gentes asked that the complaint be dropped, and so the CHRC decided not to pursue it.

Just before we were informed that the complaint had been dropped, Mark wrote the following piece about Marie-Line Gentes:

> I believe that anyone who would use a government outfit like the Canadian Human Rights Commission to silence opinions they cannot defeat by honest debate is political scum. In Canada, this kind of behaviour is encouraged by the federal government to the point that they have created and operate an agency to cater to these people.
>
> This is wrong and dangerous, but this is the way it is.

I believe all Canadians should know the name of the person who has taken this action, but she should absolutely NOT be harassed in any way. I have a very selfish motive for saying that, harassing this woman could be crossing the line into areas where we would actually be in the wrong. We have the moral and ethical high ground in this case and we don't want to damage our position by doing anything we really shouldn't do. (By 'we' I mean all FDers).

There is another issue at stake here too. Harassing people in their personal lives because of their political opinions is the hallmark of political opponents, we must be careful that we do not become that which we loathe.

I've thrown a couple of derogatory terms at Ms. Gentes myself. I was angry but I don't really feel a need to withdraw anything I've said, I owe nothing to someone who would make these kind of false accusations, not even common courtesy.

But we must be careful not to give those who would silence us legitimate ammunition. As of now they have none, we must all be careful not to hand them any.

My anger at Gentes is beginning to diminish in any case. She is not the real enemy. There will always be people like her in free societies, but as long as there are enough people who put liberty ahead of tyranny, the damage they are able to do to our country will be minimized. The real problem is that there are government organizations, paid for by the taxpayers and protected by law, that are specifically designed to do the will of these types of people.

Know your enemy. Gentes is simply an individual unable to cope with living in a free society, if anything we should feel pity for her, Canada must be a terrible place for her to have to live.

But she is not really the enemy. The enemy is a system that would allow her to use the weight of the state to harass the honest and decent people of Canada. That is the enemy we must target.

Gentes is merely a single bullet being shot at freedom, we need to remove the gun.

It was not until later that we found out that Ms. Gentes had asked for it to be dropped before the complaint was ever sent to us and that her phone call seemed to trigger a panicky rush to send us that first (allegedly second) notification.

The disclosure documents showed that she made repeated attempts to get them to discontinue and, although much is redacted, it appears the CHRC were trying to persuade her to go ahead because any comments about her online and in the media would help her case against us. Thankfully, she persisted and we never had to try to defend the impugned words in a Tribunal that had, at that time, a 100% conviction rate. Even though the impugned words were pretty mild, our odds would not have been good.

We started a celebration thread to announce that the complaint had been dropped and it was immediately overrun with anonymous posters who appeared to be up to no good. Our government buddies were in there, of course, with a huge assortment of trolls who were taking turns making racist posts and accusing us of racism. We deleted a large number of them, but left some intact after we banned the posters in case we could track down their identities at some point.

Our policeman "racist song" friend was in there, as was a guy who showed up for a real-world meeting with us later wearing a CSIS ball cap. Both of them posted comments on that thread that would later get us sued for defamation.

Our experience with the CHRC encouraged us to look deeper into what was going on there. Coincidentally, both Ezra Levant and Mark Steyn were having their own dealings with Human Rights Commissions at that point, so it shaped up into kind of a "perfect storm" where conservatives became aware and mobilized to fight against the unjust Section 13.

Early on in that fight I wrote that Section 13 was created to punish people who hadn't broken the law. My point was that it was designed for people whose comments did not reach the level of criminal hate speech, so, were it not for Section 13, the perps would walk. In fact, it was created to "get" one old guy named John Ross Taylor who keep leaving racist (but not criminally hateful) messages on his answering machine and urging people to call it.

Mark was inspired to write the following piece in December of 2007:

'The Canadian Human Rights Commission exists to punish people who haven't broken the law.' - Connie Fournier

Rarely does one sentence so perfectly describe such a complex problem as the existence of the Canadian Human Rights Commission and its various provincial counterparts. I'm proud of my wife for having spoken it, because this sentence encapsulates the political thinking behind the creation of these state organizations, along with their missions and its history to date.

There really is no way to pretty this up. The Canadian Human Rights Commission was created to punish those who haven't broken the law. It is imperative that it be understood that people like Stephen Boissoin and Scott Brockie (and many others who could, and should, be named here) did not break the law!

These people did nothing that should have involved the intervention of the State, but in today's Canada, "not breaking the law" doesn't necessarily protect anyone from being prosecuted by the State as if they were actual law breakers.

One of the most basic tenets of liberty is that people are free to do anything that isn't specifically proscribed or prohibited by law. This means we can do or say anything we want, as long as it's not already illegal. The CHRC was designed to sidestep this fundamental foundation of freedom, and it does so with alacrity. The results are atrocious.

Because the CHRC is designed to punish people who haven't broken the law, it cannot possibly operate under the legal restrictions that normally protect us from state political persecution. So it doesn't.

The *ex post facto* laws protect us from governments charging us for breaking laws before they were enacted. It prevents the State from prosecuting retroactively. However, this is exactly what the CHRC does. It takes someone's words or actions - words and actions that were entirely legal at the time they were uttered or committed - criminalizes those words and actions, and then retroactively punishes the newly created "criminals".

Another fundamental tenet of liberty is that laws must be able to be understood by the citizenry. An argument could be made that no one can understand the tax laws, but in fact there are experts who know these laws and it is our responsibility as citizens to seek out these experts when needed. The point being that there is a means at our disposal of learning what the laws are and what specifically is illegal when it comes to tax issues. Not so with CHRC operations.

There is no way for anyone to learn what is deemed to be illegal by the CHRC, because Commissioners create the laws as they go along, while prosecuting retroactively. The only way for citizens to protect themselves from attacks from the CHRC is to live in fear that any word they say or any act they may perform must first be viewed through the CHRC prism. Or remain quiet. We used to consider those kinds of actions by the State "totalitarianism". People lived in terror of the State, because they were being intimidated. For anyone who even thinks of uttering any politically incorrect thought today, the intimidation (and terror) are no less real.

Of course it's impossible to discuss the CHRC without mentioning the fact that the truth is not considered to be a defence in any case brought before this organization. This is so appallingly perverse that everyone who learns of the policy is instantly repulsed. But given the way it operates, the Commission's 100% conviction rate should surprise no one.

The CHRC was designed so people such as Marie-Line Gentes could attack her political opponents with absolutely no risk or cost to herself.

There will be no justice until the CHRC and its ilk have been dissolved and all of its cases reviewed by the public. Unjust fines should be repaid by the taxpayers, because it's the taxpayers, in the guise of "government", who were ultimately responsible for all of this happening in the first place. People who benefited personally by receiving fines should have to repay every cent to the person they received it from.

The powers that be in Ottawa appear to have no interest in putting the brakes on the CHRC, so the only defence we as citizens have against it is to educate the public as to its activities and to publish what this organization does.

Organizations such as this are photo-phobic, they have an "excessive sensitivity to light and well-lit places". In other words, they don't like light. If enough light is shed on the activities of the CHRC we can hope that it will eventually shrivel under the exposure, and perhaps justice will finally prevail. However, as with all bureaucracies, the CHRC is well-financed, and it has become powerful. It will take a lot of "light" before this organization is brought to account, and it certainly will not fade quietly into the night."

In just a few months, and, in large part due to the tenacity and thoroughness of Marc Lemire and Barbara Kulaszka, who were putting up the fiercest defence ever seen in the Canadian Human Rights Tribunal, we were learning what was wrong with the system, and we were learning to articulate why it was wrong.

When this was added to the storm, which now included other conservative bloggers like Kathy Shaidle, Arnie Lemaire and Catherine McMillan as well was politicians like Keith Martin, a few Conservative Members of Parliament, the Christian Heritage Party, the Canadian Civil Liberties Association, the BC Civil Liberties Association and PEN Canada, we had a great deal of forward momentum.

For years before this, the Canadian Human Rights Tribunal ate up people like a mulching machine. Most of these people held controversial (and mostly distasteful) political opinions so the public really didn't care what happened to them. But, for the most part, they were people of limited means who went into these Tribunals with no legal representation at all, or they just skipped the proceedings and findings were made against them.

Some of these people even went to jail for contempt of court when they ignored the standard, broad "cease and desist" order that went along with a Section 13 loss.

Mark was both horrified and fascinated by the philosophical aspect of the Section 13 problem. He continued his analysis in April of 2008 calling the Canadian Human Rights Act "contemptible" in an article where he pointed out how Section 13 was subjective and unfair.

Mark wrote:

> According to the Media Awareness Network:
> *Canada's Human Rights Act forbids behaviour that exposes a person to hatred or contempt. Specifically, section 13 of the Act makes it an offence to communicate by telephone (or to cause to be so communicated, by means of the facilities of a telecommunication undertaking) any messages likely to cause hatred or contempt.*
>
> This is an accurate summation but the closer it is examined the more convoluted, bizarre and logically contradictory it becomes.
>
> Contempt is like respect in that it cannot be produced by demand, it must be earned. The two are also similar in that the only basis people have for evaluating who deserves either is an individual's or group's actions. A thousand people could yell from the rooftops that Mother Theresa's actions were contemptible or that Paul Bernardo's actions were worthy of respect, but that would not make it so in either case. It is impossible for the Canadian Human Rights Act to be taken literally because it is internally irrational.

Because the entire *Canadian Human Rights Act* is ill-conceived, ill-considered, irrational, and downright dangerous, perverse results can be its only output. It would be impossible for a commission designed to interpret and enforce this *Act* to do its job using only ethical and legal means. Yet the CHRC does its job with appalling alacrity.

He went on later to write that justice will not be served unless the citizens who have been subjected to Section 13 complaints are fairly compensated:

How many people, in the privacy of their homes, or among trusted friends, use correctspeak? I contend that there are very few. Most of us will let our hair down when among those with whom we feel safe, and we will use terminology and express political opinions in ways we would never do in public today.

The significance of this is not that so many people do it, but in that we feel unsafe in doing it in the public square. The worst part is most of us haven't understood who is it we feel unsafe from, yet we have been conditioned to be very careful of what we say.

Citizens of a free society should be free to express their political opinions. This is so much a 'given' that to say so is to state the obvious. Yet today, many Canadians fear to speak freely and the reason for this is that we no longer live in a free society. It is unsafe for a Canadian to speak political opinions that are unapproved by the Canadian state, and it is not only unsafe for a Canadian to speak an unapproved political opinion in Canada, it is unsafe for a Canadian to do so anywhere in the world.

As a free people, we cannot allow this to stand.

The most egregious offenders of liberty in Canada today are the human rights commissions, as entities, and their staffs as individuals. These people, and the organizations that employ them, must be stopped.

Stasi-style human rights commissions must be abolished, but only as a first step.

Justice will not be served until reparations have been made to all of the human rights commissions' victims. Their kangaroo court 'convictions should be summarily overturned and any monies they have been forced to pay to these organizations should be repaid – at the expense to the taxpayer.

You will rarely see me calling for the taxpayers to have to give money to an individual, but in this case it is we taxpayers who are entirely at fault. We are the ones who allowed these commissions to be formed, we are the ones who allowed them to continue for as long as they have, we are the ones who empowered them to unjustly seize the property - and destroy the reputations and livelihoods - of innocent people. All in our names.

We cannot and should not try to avoid our own culpability.

As a freedom loving people, and as a liberty based society, we owe apologies to Scott Brockie, Stephen Boisson, Marc Lemire and many others who have had to endure abuse that should never have occurred. And we owe them money. We owe them every penny we have taken from them, we owe them every dollar they have been forced to pay to defend themselves from attacks that should never have happened, we owe them for lost careers.

And we owe it to ourselves to make sure this never happens again.

Anything less and justice will not be served.

The process of the Marc Lemire tribunal hearing became very public due to all of the high profile people who were interested in the subject. Hearing rooms that were formerly empty were suddenly filled with writers like Joseph Brean, Kady O'Malley, Mark Steyn, and as many bloggers as would fit in the room.

After the final arguments were done and the Tribunal Member, Mr. Athanasios Hadjis began his deliberations, Mark had this to say:

Connie and I came late to the Lemire case. We might not have heard of it at all if we had not ourselves been attacked by the CHRC through an absurd complaint filed by Marie-Line Gentes (a complaint that was dropped in the face of the publicity it generated.) At that point we decided to investigate our attackers and much has become public as a result.

Soon after our CHRC complaint was dropped, the human rights cases against Ezra Levant and Mark Steyn hit the news. There is a football adage that says "Defences win championships, offences sell tickets." Steyn and Levant put on a great offensive show and they sold a lot of tickets. Many Canadian eyes were opened by their to-be-aborted cases and the public "learned much that may have lay hidden." Although they may no longer have a dog in this fight, the battle goes on and the defence is back on the field.

There has been very little media attention paid to the Lemire case, yet it is one of the most far-reaching cases of our time. Many other cases, in these tribunals and in the real courts, are on hold pending Hadjis' decision in the Lemire case. When the Lemire hearings ended with Barbara Kulaszka's closing arguments in Toronto this fall, the trial of Athanasios Hadjis began.

Being a relative newcomer to human rights commissions and tribunals, I have only had two opportunities to see Mr. Hadjis in action as a tribunal chairman, both times in the Lemire case. His rulings in a number of cases are available in the public record, but I wanted to see what I could gain by direct observation. Who is this man?

From his conviction rate alone one could conclude that he is a raving ideologue, but he gives no indication of being such when he is chairing a hearing. While I could think of a number of derogatory terms for him, based on his previous rulings, after seeing him in person "fool" would not number among them. Mr. Hadjis is obviously very intelligent; he seems to be a master of the Canadian Human Rights Act, and he appears to be quite aware of the huge political forces at play around this case.

He also knows when he is being manipulated or lied to. You can see the awareness in his facial expressions and body language when a CHRC member or witness lies to him, when the CHRC alters evidence, or when a CHRC employee or witness comes down with an obvious case of selective amnesia. Yet I find this troubling. With all of this going on before his eyes, why has he consistently ruled in favour of the CHRC? Was doing so part of his unofficial job description? Was it because until recently no one was watching?

A lot of people are watching now and that completely changes the political landscape in which these tribunals operate. In the real world a prosecutor must decide whether he has enough evidence for a conviction before he approaches the courts and a judge must weigh whether his decisions will be overturned. The primary concern of these CHRC prosecutions and convictions is politics. Rather than weigh evidence and the quality of decisions, they need only weigh what they can get away with politically.

The Steyn article that was the subject of his complaint clearly violated the CHRC's in-house "Hallmarks of Hate" and it did so in a very public way, yet the commission backed away from prosecuting him. It wasn't for lack of evidence, in the world of the CHRC, they had a slam dunk case against him. They backed off because they couldn't get away with it politically and that is all that matters to an organization that is entirely political in nature.

The Lemire case began in the dark and that was where it was supposed to end, but it has already left the land of obscurity. Now it is a hot potato--of interest to the public and to legal and political communities--and it will ultimately lead to a Charter challenge of Section 13.

Athanasios Hadjis knows these things. He knows from the representation sent to the hearings from the Ministry of Justice that the Harper government wants Section 13 on the books so badly that they did a complete turnaround and read a list of reasons that Hadjis could use to dismiss the Lemire case due to abuse of process. He also has to know that if he does so he will stop the Charter challenge the Harper government so badly fears in its tracks. Mr. Hadjis also has to understand the freedoms and liberties that are at stake in this case. If he did not understand those issues when he first sat in the Chair, he surely does now.

The pressure on Mr. Hadjis is huge and it is coming from many quarters. What will he do?

When the Lemire hearings ended the trial of Athanasios Hadjis began.

We can only await the outcome.

When Mr. Hadjis finally came out with his ruling on September 2, 2009, Ezra Levant said it was "a great day for freedom of speech". He went on, "Athanasios Hadjis didn't just throw out the case against Marc Lemire, he threw out the law, too, calling it an infringement of the free speech guarantees of the Charter of Rights." Mark Steyn called it "A Landmark Victory".

Unfortunately, the CHRC appealed the decision and ultimately won when the Federal Court of Appeal found Section 13 to be constitutional. But, not before Brian Storseth introduced Bill C-304 to repeal Section 13. It passed and that "contemptible" law was removed from the Canadian Human Rights Act.

So many people were responsible for winning this fight for our freedom of speech. Nobody more than Marc Lemire and Barbara Kulaszka who fought for years and provided all of the statistics and information we needed to get to the public to turn the tide. But, there was a huge groundswell of support from the conservative side of the political spectrum. They beat on the drum for as long as it took because they were fighting for principles that were near and dear to their hearts.

We were fighting for freedom of speech for everyone, even those with opinions contrary to our own. We were fighting for due process. We were fighting against legislation that was ambiguous and subjective. We were fighting against a system that penalized defendants by providing free legal counsel for the other side. We were fighting against a system where 100% of the defendants were found guilty. We were fighting against tribunal hearings being held behind closed doors. We were fighting against secret government disruption of private citizen's websites.

All of these things were principles that we held to be critical to the health of a democratic society. We fought for those principles, and we won.

7. THE LONG GUN REGISTRY

NOBODY has arrested us and we want to know why," Bruce Montague said to the Niagara Falls Review. "With such an expensive, fancy new law, you think they'd be willing to take it for a spin around the block."

It was July 2003 and Bruce and four other members of the Canadian Unregistered Firearms Association (CUFA) were on a speaking tour, hoping to get arrested. They wanted to be arrested because they wanted the opportunity to challenge in court the controversial long gun registry.

Mr. Montague said that it was unconstitutional. According to the Niagara Falls Review, CUFA stated the following:

> ...The Firearms Act violates the Canadian Charter of Rights and Freedoms, specifically rights to privacy, security of person, presumption of innocence, association, representation, mobility and freedom from unreasonable search and seizure. By

registering their guns, they would be complying with these personal infringements.

The interesting thing is that, in political circles, there are a lot of people who swear they would go to prison to defend their rights. We saw it ourselves when we were first notified of the Section 13 complaint against us. There were the posters who swore to stand by us no matter what it took, even if they went to prison. There were also a few who encouraged us to ignore the complaint and stand up for their rights even if it meant us going to prison! But, in the end, as is usually the case, nobody went to prison over the Free Dominion human rights complaint. Thankfully it wasn't required because nobody really wanted to pay that kind of a price if they didn't have to.

I haven't talked to Bruce Montague lately but I've often wondered if he regrets the path that he took back then. After all, he was one of the leading players in raising public awareness of the long gun registry, so it is likely that his actions contributed immensely to the final repeal of the registry. But Bruce Montague was forced to pay a personal price that I'm sure is way beyond what he even imagined.

Bruce was arrested on September 11, 2004. His wife Donna was also arrested.

There was a Charter Trial, since he claimed that the long gun registry violated the Charter of Rights, and a Criminal Trial. Both of those took place in the fall and winter of 2007. This was a year and a half after Stephen Harper became Prime Minister. The Charter challenge was rejected and, in the end, Bruce was sentenced to 18 months in prison and Donna was given probation. They both now have criminal records.

But, it didn't end there. Since Bruce Montague was a gunsmith and he sold and repaired guns, his life savings were tied up in his stock. The value of the weapons and ammunition, he estimated at about $100,000. The government, again under the watch of the Harper government, sought to seize it all, and they won. Bruce and Donna begged the court to allow a third person to sell the inventory and give them the value since they were no longer allowed to own them, but they were simply taken and not returned.

Now, the Ontario government is attempting to seize the Montague family home under the law that permits the seizure of "proceeds of crime". The Canadian Constitutional Foundation is representing them and they are accepting donations for their legal fight. It is a good cause, and a way to help a family that has already paid more in the fight for our freedom than most of us ever will.

The long gun registry was something that Free Dominion members were tuned in to from the very beginning. In January 2002, Mark wrote, 'An individual's position on gun control reveals his political soul."

This was part of a conversation during the leadership race between Stephen Harper and Stockwell Day. During one of the debates it had come to light that Harper had, in fact, voted for the long gun registry on its second reading. When asked about it, he said that at the time he felt his constituents wanted him to vote that way. He went on to state his position on the gun registry as this, "As Leader of the Official Opposition I will use all the powers afforded to me as Leader and continue our party's fight to repeal Bill C-68 and replace it with a firearms control system that is cost effective and respects the rights of Canadians to own and use firearms responsibly."

Several posters were uncomfortable with that statement and said that they did not want to trade one yoke for another. If he was going to repeal Bill C-68, they did not want him to replace it with another "firearms control system". Some even started to refer to him as a "gun grabber".

In one public statement, Stephen Harper quoted Gary Breitkreuz, a Canadian Alliance Member of Parliament who had been very outspoken about the long gun registry. This is a great quote because he clearly outlines the principles that were violated by Bill C-68. These were the reasons we were fighting:

> While the gun registry is likely the most costly and useless part of Bill C-68, it is hardly the most objectionable. Bill C-68 trampled fundamental property rights. Bill C-68 breached the privacy rights of at least 3.5 million Canadians without their knowledge. Bill C-68 placed in jeopardy our charter rights to be secure against unreasonable search and seizure. Bill C-68 eliminated our right to remain silent. Bill C-68 reversed the onus of proof, thereby eliminating our rights to be presumed innocent until proven guilty. It infringes on the treaty rights of aboriginal people. It intrudes unnecessarily into the exclusive constitutional jurisdiction of the provinces over property and civil rights, health, safety and education.

In April of 2012, the long gun registry was scrapped. The Montagues won their fight, although it was undoubtedly not in the way they expected to win it.

Still, though, they paid a terrible personal price for standing up for their convictions. The Harper government needs to own their part in that, and gun owners need to hold them accountable.

8. CONSERVATIVE ATTACKS ON THE INTERNET

ALTHOUGH Free Dominion members had been working hard to hold the leadership of the Canadian Alliance/Conservative Party accountable over the years, and we had repeatedly expressed our frustration as we were seeing power concentrated in the office of the Leader/Prime Minister, we were still trying to work within the framework of the party to get the changes we wanted.

We may have been naive - perhaps we over-estimated the commitment of the party leadership to grassroots populism, and perhaps we over-estimated the power of our own voices. We knew they were listening. We could see them responding in real time by sending their own operatives into the forum and participating in the dialogue. We honestly felt like we could make a difference.

Although we threw up our hands at times over the top-down approach favoured by Stephen Harper, it never occurred to us to be frightened of him. We knew he left something to be desired as the leader of our party because he was so controlling. But, we were willing to give him the benefit of the doubt because we knew that trying to lead a bunch of opinionated conservatives was a bit like herding cats. We weren't happy, but we didn't think it was a problem we couldn't fix internally. In fact, when the party leadership election took place in 2004, pitting Stephen Harper against Belinda Stronach and Tony Clement, most Free Dominion members supported Harper. Never for a second did we think that the man Stephen Harper would actually carry it so far that the very democratic nature of our country would be threatened by his actions.

We were the "good guys"! We were going to send our leader in there to clean up the mess left by those awful Liberals! Canada was going to have a government that was open and accountable and transparent. There would be no embarrassing scandals like AdScam. Our government wouldn't spend a billion dollars on something designed to invade the privacy of Canadians like the Liberals did with the long gun registry! Stephen Harper wasn't perfect; he was just doing what he had to do to get elected. When he became Prime Minister, everything would change!

We worked extremely hard to get the Conservative Party elected in 2006. We were elated! The time had come for our principles to be enacted in Ottawa. We just knew that once Canadians discovered how open and honest our government was, and how, for the first time, they actually had a voice in the House of Commons, they would be just as happy as we were.

There is a saying that the definition of insanity is to keep doing the same thing over and over expecting different results. Well, I guess we were subject to a kind of group insanity that drove us to push Stephen Harper's past actions out of our minds and keep expecting that he would suddenly start following the party policy that the grassroots members worked so hard to create.

It is telling that, in the summer of July 2009, when Jesse Kline wrote a piece for the Western Standard called, "Government of Canada moves to monitor Internet users", the reaction of posters in the forum was utter shock that he had gone this far. One member wrote, "Did anybody here attend the CPC Policy Convention where this proposal to monitor the Internet was introduced, debated and approved? Must have missed it."

I can hear our political opponents scoffing at us for our naivety, and I can completely understand the anger that the left must be feeling because this was *us*. This was our doing. We chose him as our leader. We enabled him when we should have dumped him for refusing to follow party policy. And, then we actually helped to elect him so that he had charge of our entire country. We worked for all of those years with the best of intentions, thinking how good our country would be once our leader was in a position to bring our kind of democratic freedom to Canada. What we did instead was unleash on our country a man who would do anything for power.

We should have realized before July, 2009 that we were in pretty deep trouble. We were actually complaining a lot more loudly as we saw that our policies were not being enacted. But, the Conservative Party trolls who appeared when we started to complain too much gave us the same canned responses every time. "You are being unreasonable." "You aren't being team players." "You aren't giving Stephen Harper a chance." And, the biggest silencing gun of all, "He can't do anything if he doesn't have a majority, so be quiet or you will jeopardize all of the work we've done to this point."

Some of us griped that that was just an excuse and that we knew that if he got his majority those same trolls would simply come back and tell us that he couldn't act because he might lose his majority. But, we really didn't have a lot of real options to affect the change that was needed.

On June 18 of 2007, the Western Standard published an article talking about how Free Dominion members had actually started to have meetings about creating a new Reform Party. It was that bad, and we knew it. We had reached the point where we knew for sure that our voices and our policies were inconsequential to our party leader.

In retrospect, I don't think it is all that surprising that exactly one month after that Western Standard article was published, we received a Section 13 complaint in the mail, and our lives have been completely consumed with defending ourselves ever since. Disrupted.

Despite all of this, when I speak of the shock we felt when we were first introduced to the Investigative Powers for the 21st Century Act, I am not exaggerating. As angry as we were at being silenced within the party, we never thought that Stephen Harper would attempt to use the same kind of control tactics on the entire country.

The proposed act was to require Internet Service Providers (ISPs) to install equipment that would intercept all of their traffic and save the browsing history of all of their customers, and allow police to obtain subscriber information (names, addresses, emails, etc.) from ISPs without a warrant.

Some of the comments left by Free Dominion members were blistering in nature. "I wonder if the Harper supporters still want us to believe that if we give the Cons a majority they will stand for freedom. I can't believe how incredibly stupid I was in helping this party get into office. I cringe with embarrassment when I think of it," was the comment by one poster.

The next person chimed in with, "We need to get rid of Harper and his gang of liberals! Time for some real conservatism in our lives. Uh oh... my door bell just rang... wonder if it's the RCMP coming to take me away for my thoughts?!" Another one read, "In the years I foolishly supported the conservatives I heard lefties talk about "hidden agendas" and that they were "closet fascists". Turns out..."

I started another thread on this issue and wrote the following:

> Our Conservative government thinks that they have the right to strip every single citizen in this country of their online anonymity.
>
> This time we have to do more than sit back and whine and complain about it.
>
> I obviously don't agree with 'outing' individuals, but I have no problem 'outing' pseudonyms that belong to CPC operatives.
>
> My proposal is that, if this government insists on doing this, we strip them of their anonymity, too.
>
> Every blogger and forum owner in Canada should begin compiling a list of usernames that have been used by IP addresses owned by

the Conservative Party of Canada or the House of Commons, and we should set a day for a collective "reveal".

These people have had no problem using FD and sites like it as a free vehicle for their Party propaganda. Why should they have the advantage of distancing themselves from their own anonymous comments when they are trying to take that freedom away from us?

Free Dominion hasn't saved IP addresses for well over a year, but the old ones are still there. No *individuals* can be outed as a result of this because we won't reveal full IP addresses and, unlike these government officials under the proposed new law, we don't have access to names and addresses associated with IP addresses.

But, if the Harper government wants the power to "out" any Canadian for any reason, then they can jolly well own the comments of their own operatives."

After I posted the above rant, several other bloggers commented on the thread and expressed their support for the idea. Eventually it was decided that the "outing" of the government operatives would take place after the bill became law because then we could out the operatives of the parties of that voted for it.

As it turned out, Stephen Harper decided to prorogue Parliament shortly after they returned for their fall session in 2009 so this iteration of the Investigative Powers for the 21st Century Act died on the order paper and Internet users breathed a sigh of relief.

Before that, though, in November of 2009, Rob Nicholson introduced another bill which he claimed was to target child pornography.

The bill pushed required ISPs to monitor their users and report any material of a sexual nature that involved minors. They were also to preserve the evidence. Failure to comply would result in large fines and prison terms for ISP owners.

At the time, I wrote this:

People who produce and distribute child pornography should be shot in the head. But, creating a law that requires ISPs to spy on their clients or risk prison time is a dangerous, dangerous thing.

Notice how these internet bills keep coming from the Conservative Party? They can't STAND internet privacy.

Rob Nicholson has seriously got to go."

I continued in the post below:

Do you have any idea how easy it would be to set up a webmaster or an internet service provider using this legislation? And, how easily it could be expanded to include other categories of postings?

How many Canadians are going to want to provide blogs or forums when it is a money-losing proposition that opens you up to human rights complaints, defamation suits, and now prison time if your posters cross the line?

The Conservatives are on a rampage against freedom of expression and privacy on the internet.

And, the party faithful yawn....."

Other posters agreed that this legislation was short-sighted and frightening. I said, "But, this legislation gives me the creeps. Nobody should have to face a prison sentence over the actions of someone else. And, ISPs should not be forced to spy on clients who are not even under suspicion."

Given that the Investigative Powers for the 21st Century Act was still in Committee, waiting to be passed, and the government was already putting this Internet bill forward, too, we began to notice a disturbing pattern.

One poster said, "In my worst nightmares I would never have believed that a party which "calls itself conservative" would become the government that champions a true Police State....and people want these thugs to have a majority?"

I commented:

What the Conservative government is doing is providing one more major disincentive for Canadians webmasters. Whether it is intentional or not, the result will be less online speech opportunities for Canadians. Unfortunately, I think it is quite intentional.

This bill also died when Parliament was prorogued that year, but it wasn't the end of it.

The next year, after the introduction of more Internet legislation, I decided to take a day and go to the

House of Commons website to see exactly what legislation had been introduced by this government, what was sitting there waiting to passed, and what horrors were in store for our privacy and freedom of speech.

I entitled my post, "Harper Conservatives' relentless attack on the Internet", because that is exactly what I found on the House of Commons website.

I wrote:

Whether you know it or not, we have a very, very serious problem in Canada right now. As you will see shortly, our government has been chipping away at our Internet freedom and privacy in an alarming way. If this doesn't stop, Canadian cyberspace is going to be as tightly controlled as our television and radio airspace under the CRTC.

Alarm bells have been going off for me for awhile now, but even I was shocked when I took all of the government bills regarding the Internet and put them in one place. Our freedom is in grave peril!

I listed them:

1. **Bill C-22** *An Act respecting the mandatory reporting of Internet child pornography by persons who provide an Internet service (Protecting Children from Online Sexual Exploitation Act)* **Introduced** **by:** Rob Nicholson
   Status: Passed first reading on May 6, 2010
   Details: This was a reintroduction of Bill C-58 that had died in 2009.

2. **Bill C-27** *An Act to promote the efficiency and adaptability of the Canadian economy by regulating certain activities that discourage reliance on electronic means of carrying out commercial activities, and to amend the Canadian Radio-television and Telecommunications Commission Act, the Competition Act, the Personal Information Protection and Electronic Documents Act and the Telecommunications Act*
(*Electronic Commerce Protection Act*)

Introduced by: Tony Clement
Status: Passed Third Reading, Reintroduced on May 25, 2010 after prorogue
Details: The ECPA designates the CRTC as the main regulatory agency responsible for pursuing administrative penalties against those who violate the Act (clause 14). The CRTC is given numerous powers in relation to this mandate, including the right to cause a demand to be served on a telecommunications provider to verify compliance with the ECPA, and to prevent disclosure of that demand for the purposes of protecting an investigation (clause 15).(19) The telecommunications provider, which is required to preserve data for the purposes of complying with the demand, is entitled to apply for a review if either the preservation of data or non-disclosure would place an undue burden upon it (clause 16).

The CRTC also has the power to require that a person produce a document in his or her possession or control, or to require preparation of a document based on data, information or documents in the possession or control of that person (clause 17). Again, anyone subject to such a requirement has the right to apply for review on the grounds of unreasonableness or the possibility of disclosing privileged information, or to seek conditions on the disclosure (clause 18). The CRTC may also apply to a justice of the peace for a warrant to enter a place of business pursuant to the ECPA, and unless the warrant contains different conditions, may then examine anything found there, use any means of communication found there, and examine or use any computer systems, documents, and copying equipment found there. It may also remove, for copying or examination, anything found at the place it has entered, and it may prohibit or limit access to the place itself. The owner of the place is required to give all reasonably required assistance to the CRTC under such circumstances (clause 19).

3. **Bill C-47** *An Act regulating telecommunications facilities to support investigations (Technical Assistance for Law Enforcement in the 21st Century Act)*

   Introduced by: Peter Van Loan
   Status: Passed second reading, died in committee due to prorogue
   Details: Technical Assistance for Law Enforcement in the 21st Century Act (Bill C-47) will require Internet Service Providers (ISP's) and other "telecommunications service providers" to install equipment facilitating the interception of communications, and to allow police access, without a warrant, to the personal information of users including names, addresses, telephone numbers, email addresses and internet protocol addresses.

4. Section 16 of the Technical Assistance for Law Enforcement in the 21st Century Act provides that the Commissioner of the Royal Canadian Mounted Police, the Director of the Canadian Security Intelligence Service and the head of a police service constituted under the laws of a province may designate a limited number of persons who may request particular personal information from a telecommunications service provider.

5. **Bill C-46** *Investigative Powers for the 21st Century Act An Act to amend the Criminal Code, the Competition Act and the Mutual Legal Assistance in Criminal Matters Act*
   Introduced by: Rob Nicholson
   Status: Passed second reading, in committee, died due to prorogation
   Details: At the time, Michael Geist wrote on his blog, "It is pretty much exactly what law enforcement has been demanding and privacy groups have been fearing. It represents a reneging of a commitment from the previous Public Safety Minister on court oversight and will embed broad new surveillance capabilities in the Canadian Internet."

6. **Bill C-58** *An Act respecting the mandatory reporting of Internet child pornography by persons who provide an Internet service (Child Protection Act (Online Sexual Exploitation))*
   Introduced by: Rob Nicholson
   Status: Passed second reading, died in committee due to prorogue
   Details: This was the bill that died in 2009. At the time Michael Geist wrote on his blog, "This bill marks the second piece of legislation this

year that opens the door to far greater ISP policing and monitoring of their networks. ISPs are quietly being deputized as law enforcement assistants, with new requirements to install surveillance capabilities and provide information on their subscribers and their activities."

7. **Bill C-21** *An Act to amend the Canadian Human Rights Act*
   Introduced by: Chuck Strahl
   Status: Royal Assent
   Details: This Act removed the section of the Canadian Human Rights Act that exempted people under the Indian Act. Basically, Canadians who were fortunate enough to have protection from Section 13 can now be targets. In the beginning of the fight against Section 13, this is the Bill that MPs were told to refer to if constituents asked about CHRA reform. That evasive "talking points" memo created a stir on the Internet at the time.

8. **Bill C-61** *An Act to amend the Copyright Act*
   Introduced by: Jim Prentice
   Status: First Reading, Being reintroduced with an intent to be passed in June
   Details: It was unclear at that time exactly what this bill would contain, but experts expected users to lose several "fair use" rights as a result.

9. **Bill C-44** *An Act to amend the Canadian Human Rights Act*
   Introduced by: Jim Prentice
   Status: Died in Committee
   Details: Reintroduced as C-21 (see above)

I then provided a quick summary of what the combined legislation had done (or would do):

- Native Canadians have lost their immunity from the CHRA (like Section 13).

- Internet service providers will have to install spy software to monitor their customers' activities.

- Internet service providers will have to turn over the information they collect to police, CSIS etc. without a warrant.

- Internet service providers, forum owners, blog owners etc will be forced to monitor ALL use of their services (even private correspondence) because they will be held responsible if someone uses their services for child pornography and they don't report it.

- The CRTC will be given power to demand information from internet service providers and impose penalties on Canadians for copyright violations. (The CRTC has wanted power over the internet for years, and the Conservatives are handing it to them).

- Canadians may be investigated and fined for copying their own music onto their computers.

- Internet service providers will be allowed to "throttle" traffic if they suspect the users are downloading copyrighted files.

- Canadians could be fined for tinkering with their own electronics.

• Without a warrant, police will be able to "remotely activate existing tracking devices that are found in certain types of technologies such as cell phones".

These Internet bills kept popping up regularly over the next couple of years. They were like weeds. Sometimes they would die when Parliament ended, but they were always reintroduced. This government was absolutely determined to get control of the Internet.

Around the same time a site called News1130 reported that the government was monitoring and responding to conversations in the social media.

They said:

A company out of Toronto, called Social Media Group, was paid $75,000 to help counter information put out by the anti-sealing movement.

The company tells the government what it considers to be 'questionable statements,' government employees then reply with information. Some experts say the Tories monitoring the public was just a matter of time.

Although it was galling to think that the government was actually paying people to do this, the fact that it was being done was, of course, no surprise to us on Free Dominion. Government employees and operatives had been participating in the forum since day one.

One of the most memorable fights that we had was against Bill C-30. This was another iteration of a lawful access bill and it was introduced by Vic Toews. Its original title was "The Lawful Access Act", but, in a cynically calculating move, it was changed to "Protecting Children from Internet Predators Act".

One of the things about this bill that drew criticism on Free Dominion was the fact that it gave these powers to "police, CSIS, and the Competition Bureau." It was never explained how giving surveillance powers to the Competition Bureau would protect Canadians from child pornographers.

A Free Dominion member posted that excerpt from the bill and said, "What happened to the conservative movement in Canada? We need a movement in place to act as a counter-balance."

But, overall, this bill was pretty similar to the Investigative Powers for the 21st Century Act; it was just re-branded as a bill "for the children".

Vic Toews famously drew the wrath of the Internet community when he responded to a Liberal MP who opposed the bill: "He can either stand with us or with the child pornographers."

A Free Dominion member fumed, "Who writes these bills ... and why didn't the minister in charge read this bill before issuing moral ultimatums to Canadians?"

OpenMedia organized a fight against the bill and entitled it "Stop Spying". And, Twitter exploded in opposition as well. Someone created a Twitter hashtag called #TellVicEverything. The idea was that he obviously wanted to know everything about our lives, so we might as well just tell him. People used that hashtag and hilariously provided him the mundane details of their day, from what they ate for breakfast to what they were doing at that instant in time. One person lamented that he had lost a copy of a document he was working on and asked Vic to send him the copy he had of it.

Things took a darker turn when someone started posting embarrassing excerpts from Toews divorce documents with the suggestion that if he believes citizens shouldn't have privacy, then neither should he.

In the end, the lawful access provisions were removed from the child pornography bill, so the Internet was given a reprieve. It was a brief one.

The final battle for Lawful Access came in 2014 when Peter MacKay rebranded it, yet again, as a bill against "cyber-bullying." In the face of massive opposition, the government pushed forward. Even when Carol Todd, mother of one of Canada's most well-known victims of cyber-bullying, stepped forward to express her concerns about this legislation, it fell on deaf ears. When the Supreme Court made a ruling that rendered the parts of the bill that allowed warrantless access unconstitutional, they still would not consider backing down again.

In March of 2015, Bill C-15 came into effect and the privacy of innocent Canadians became another casualty in the Harper government's relentless quest for unlimited power.

9. BILL C-51 - THE ANTI-TERRORISM ACT, 2015

I have called Bill C-51, The Anti-Terrorism Act of 2015, the worst piece of legislation I have ever seen. This is not an exaggeration. In fact, I struggle to think of another bill in my lifetime that has been so universally rejected. And, the people who have rejected it are the people with the knowledge and experience to understand exactly what impact this legislation will have on our lives.

Many people, including law professors (100 of them signed one open letter), privacy experts, privacy commissioners, former CSIS agents, judges and business leaders have expressed their serious concern over the information sharing provisions in the bill. Law professors Craig Forcese and Kent Roach wrote a paper on the bill and they said that the unaccountable information sharing between some 17 government departments including CRA, CSIS, CSE, RCMP, as well as with others as they so choose, amounts to a situation that is tantamount to "total information awareness.". It basically eviscerates our privacy laws by allowing sharing of very personal data such as our tax information. But, it becomes even more ominous when you consider the combined effect of this law with Bill C-13, which greatly expanded the government's ability to gather information on citizens. It will create unknown numbers of databases of our information with no oversight regarding who gets their hands on it.

I've heard many times during this debate about the privacy aspects of this bill that, "If you have nothing to hide, you have nothing to fear." But, this isn't about wanting to hide things about ourselves for nefarious purposes, this is about maintaining the human dignity of conducting our lives without being constantly watched. It's a freedom issue. If you would not be comfortable with someone posting all of your emails or text messages or your tax returns online for the world to see, then you have reason to worry about the sharing of information that is allowed under this law. We all have conversations with friends and family about deeply personal aspects of our lives. Sometimes we do this in text form. In a free society, we should not have to be worrying that someday those conversations will be passed around between government offices and analyzed, dissected, and shared.

As a society we have long agreed it is wrong to open someone else's mail. With the combination of lawful access legislation and Bill C-51, it is like consenting to having all your mail opened, copied and stored forever so that it can be read if you ever pop up on the government radar. When discussing this bill I asked the following rhetorical question:

> Imagine for a moment if you are an opposition MP and the government has the power to collect and freely distribute all of the private information they can obtain about you.

Do you think it would be used against you? Or do you think that if you have nothing to hide you have nothing to fear?

In addition to information sharing, the law gives permission to government agents such as CSIS operatives to "disrupt" targets that they are investigating. Disruption has such a broad interpretation in the bill that they found it necessary to stipulate that those agents were not allowed to rape us or kill us.

While Bill C-51 was being debated, I wrote the following about "disruption":

> [Disruption] is a word that was used in a "Five Eyes" PowerPoint presentation that was released some time ago by Edward Snowden. The "Five Eyes" countries include Canada, the USA, Great Britain, Australia and New Zealand. This presentation was given to the Joint Threat Research Intelligence Group and it was entitled, "The Art of Deception: Training for Online Covert Operations.

> This PowerPoint presentation talks about how government agents can go about sabotaging online groups that they want silenced. These groups need not be criminals or terrorists, they simply describe them as "hacktivists". These documents call this activity "Online Covert Action", and say it consists of the "3 D's" - Deny, Disrupt, Degrade, Deceive. One of the documents outright declares that they are "pushing the boundaries" when they speak of deliberately destroying their targets' reputations, infiltrating groups and using psychology to "disrupt" them, and in manipulating and controlling the information that is posted online."

In an open letter to the National Post, 100 law professors made the point that, under Bill C-51, judges would now be expected to issue warrants for "disruption" measures that might contravene the law, or the Charter Rights of the target. They can even order other people to violate the rights of their fellow Canadians and forbid them from telling the target.

These hearings would be held without the presence, input or knowledge of the target, and the target would not likely ever know that the hearing had taken place so there would be no legal recourse (such as an appeal) if an unjust decision was made.

They also pointed out that the term "terrorist" was so broadly defined as to make it almost meaningless. These tactics could be used against virtually any Canadian who was on the wrong side of the government of the day.

Speaking to conservatives I have repeatedly urged them to consider the potential impact of this legislation on their lives should one of the other parties gain control of Parliament. The people who purport such distrust for Justin Trudeau and Thomas Mulcair should be frightened to death of the thought of them with the powers of "disruption" in their hands.

We know quite a bit about government "disruption" from the history of Free Dominion. It was actually alarming to read the Five Eyes presentation as we could see that some of those tactics had actually been used against us.

It took us a long time to realize that many of the people who were repeatedly posting things on Free Dominion that were inflammatory, outrageous, racist, or embarrassing to the site, were actually people with access to government computers (as evidenced by their IP addresses).

When we were debating lawful access, I threatened to "out" those people if the Conservative Party chose to take away our privacy, but, until now, I haven't done so. That is mostly because it is such a huge job to find them all!

But, for the sake of illustration in this book, I think it is important that people understand the kind of stuff that government employees/agents were posting on our site over the years. So, I've compiled a very short list as an example of that material. You can see how these posts could cause harm to our reputation, cause dissension amongst forum posters, and manipulate the message. Many of these comments could even have left us, as publishers, liable for defamation or Section 13 complaints. ([sic] throughout.)

- I am new here but think it could be a communications disaster if it ever went to press that US based funds were in support of FD, resulting in a great loss of legitimacy which you may need in future if and when the tide turns from the current liberal extremism.

- I think it's fair to ask how Steve Harper turned into Stephen Harper. Stephen Harper, Reform MP, said much the same thing. Stephen Harper of the NCC said much the same thing.

- http://recallharper.theblog.net/

- WHY WAS THE QUEBEC NATION A WHIPPED VOTE? WHY DID NOT ONE CONSERVATIVE MP VOTE NO?

- What's grass roots about the CPC?

- It'll be awfully embarassing if it ever turns out that reporters ever fed Conservative MP's questions....

- Bulldog and company you almost make it sound like there are no CPC MPs who might threaten the virtue of HOC pages of either sex, heterosexually or not.

- So you folks really expect a gay politician [John Baird] to come out against SSM marriage? Umm, good luck with that.

- [On Cretien being PM] Actually, that would mean that drooling retards (oh sorry, I mean "special needs" folks) who can't string a sentence together are also PM material.

- I think ultimately we'll be looking at another PC/Reform type of split within the party like what happened with Mulroney. Why? Because the West will want out, like you rightfully point out. I just feel it's inevitable.

- [On Deb Grey riding a motorcycle] Seems like a dykie thing to do. Not that there's anything WRONG with that, of course.

- Does CPAC add more than the average 10 pounds that tv is supposed to add? Egghead JImbo Moore looks like he's tipping the scales at about 350 lbs nowadays. They had to break out the wide angle lens on his head.

- THANK GOD! We don't be needin no queers on this board! :lol:
  "I'm Rudy with a Survivor plight.

And I gots this feeling I'm in trouble tonight.
My ass will be a target I fear,
Because I'm living on an island full of QUEERS!
I gots queers to the left of me,
Lezzies to the right,
'Cause I'm stuck on an island with queers
Yeah I'm stuck on an island with queers..."

- No I don't think your wife will let you go see Harper - especially once she finds out how big and luscious his man-titties are.

- Solution: turn the CPC into a White European Christian defender party

- I'd love if the latter hypothesis is true. Telling Western women that they'll get breast cancer if they don't reproduce... there couldn't be anything better.

- "Cultural conservatives" understand that when we treat all cultures as equally "Canadian" (or "American" or "British"), we cease to have a culture at all, and lose all sense of our roots, our identity, and our values.

- "Racialist conservatives" want Whites, who underwent seperated evolution 100 thousand years ago, to live in isolation, because they know we will disappear otherwise. They believe that the biological make-up of Europeans was helpful in the construction and perpetuation of the above two social constructs.

- Jews, and only Jews in my opinion, have the power to destroy the New World Order - to break the psychological link European Christianity, academia, and the MSM have between nationalism and nazism.

- The White ethnic group is a recessive (phenotypically) ethnic group in comparison to the Black, Brown Caucassion, and Oriental ethnic groups. Within a relatively short period of time in the future, we'll cease to exist.

- Less talk; more action. Join the Separation Party of Alberta today: http://www.separationalberta.com/join.asp

- It's you who is the coward and weakling who won't stand up for TRUE CONSERVATISM who won't stand up FOR HIS PEOPLE! YOU ARE A NEO-CON. TRAITOR! TRAITOR! YOU HAVE FORSAKENED YOUR PEOPLE, YOUR CHILDREN AND YOUR GRANDCHILDREN. NONE OF WHAT YOU DO HELPS US NEO-CON! TAKE THAT TO THE GRAVE COWARD!

- Guess what...I am having sex regularly, today with a female nordic caucasoid...in the past with mongoloids and nigroids (this is actually the politically correct racial name for Black)... as well as caucasoids (prettiest)

- I didn't want to annoy the board with another thread on 'European' ethnic group issues, so I put this here: High suicide rate for older white males

- God I envy the First Nations ... give me a reserve, a place where my kind alone exists, a place to celebrate our way of life, ... and I have happiness.

- The Islamic cancer will spread until it is too late...why don't people see that??? Their population is increasing everywhere and they are slowly voting in their political preference.

- Layton shut your welfare receiving, bottom feeding, trough sucking kiss hole, you piece of social shyte.

- I'm sorry but I cannot recall one islamic person who has done anything substantial for modern mankind, be it medicine, science, arts or humanities. can you?

As you can see from this, and from the other examples we have given of attempts to smear us elsewhere, we were fighting a battle that we didn't even fully understand at the time. Even without the unfettered mandate of Bill C-51 to "disrupt" us, there has certainly been an attempt to cause division in the membership, to cause moderation issues for Mark, myself, and the moderators, and to hurt the reputation of both the site, and of Mark, and me, personally.

Consider that the vast majority of the disruption we have experienced has been under the watch of a Conservative government. Yes, we have been a thorn in the side of Stephen Harper at times, but only because we take our conservative principles seriously. The fact that these kinds of disruptive acts took place against a conservative website with the Conservative Party at the helm, shows clearly that nobody is safe.

I shudder to think of what forms of "disruption" will come our way now that Bill C-51 has become law. Maybe the site will just disappear someday. Maybe our computers will be hacked, or the government will find some dirt on someone we are close to, or they will order people to cyber-stalk us, or they'll interfere with our employment. I would go further, but you get the idea, and there is no point in supplying them with evil plans of my own making!

When I was writing about Bill C-51 before it was passed I urged conservatives to ask themselves the following questions, and I think we should still consider them.

1) Do you trust government operatives to handle their open-ended freedom to "disrupt" us in a responsible way?

2) Do you think that you can trust every future Prime Minister to use these new powers in a way that is not abusive?

3) Are you comfortable with government agencies having the right to share your private information with anyone they please for any reason? And, lastly,

4) are you comfortable with the fact that the power to disrupt us is so broad that the writers of this bill felt it was necessary to stipulate that agents aren't allowed to rape or kill us?

Clearly, my answer to all four of those questions is a resounding, "No.".

10. PRINCIPLES MATTER

IT was important, I think, to revisit the battles against Section 13 and the long gun registry because it brings us back to our roots. We did not fight against those issues simply because they were Liberal laws. In fact, Section 13 was Brian Mulroney's baby. We fought them because they violated principles that we, as conservatives, hold dear.

Section 13 was an assault on our freedom of speech. It sacrificed the very real right of freedom of expression for some imaginary "right" not to be offended. The definition of "hate" was so broad that it made the application completely subjective and unfair. It was an affront to due process. Hearings took place in a tribunal instead of a regular court where basic defences like "truth" and "intent" were not accepted. The complainants' interests were represented in these hearings by legal counsel for the Canadian Human Rights Commission so they did not need to provide their own counsel. Defendants, on the other hand, had to hire a lawyer or represent themselves. If the Defendant won (which was virtually impossible, anyway), there was no provision for them to get their money back. In addition, there were incidents of inappropriate spying and disruption behaviour, including Commission Employees taking on pseudonyms like Dean Steacy's "jadewarr" to sign up on forums they were investigating, and over a dozen Commission employees emailing and gossiping about their targets.

It is easy to see how the exact same issues we were protesting here are very much alive in Conservative lawful access legislation and Bill C-51.

Freedom of speech is threatened in Bill C-51. The Canadian Journalists for Free Expression (CJFE) put it this way:

> Under the bill, internet service providers and telecom providers would be required to remove any content that a judge considers terrorist propaganda, as well as anything that makes terrorist propaganda available.

The definition of "terrorist" in Bill C-51 is so broad that it makes its application completely subjective and unfair.

Truth and intent are not a defence. CJFE continues, "Linking to a video from a group like ISIS or Boko Haram could be blocked and taken down from your web and social media sites – even if you condemn the materials in your post."

Instead of a defendant simply being denied the right to have a real trial, and having to bear his own legal costs, Bill C-51 allows for secret hearings where the defendant will not even be aware - much less allowed to present evidence in his/her own defence. And, judges, hearing evidence from only one side, can permit the violation of the target's Charter Rights. The judge can even order others to violate the defendant's rights and never tell.

Bill C-51 specifically allows for all kinds of "disruption" of the target. Government agents can freely spy on websites, sign up and cause trouble, and spy the way the CHRC was doing under Section 13. But now they will have even more freedom. In fact, they will be able to do virtually anything but rape or kill you.

The Conservative Party, who made such a big deal about doing the principled thing and repealing Section 13, has created an absolute monster to replace it. Bill C-51 is not just similar to Section 13, it is a thousand times worse and it must be opposed for the same reasons we opposed its predecessor.

The gun registry is another law that we fought for good reasons. It violated our privacy rights. And, it created a government database of information that was insecure. It was expensive - a billion dollar boondoggle.

Conservative lawful access legislation has given the government the authority to gather more information on citizens than C-68 ever thought to ask for. Our privacy rights are now being violated in unprecedented ways as innocent citizens are being watched by a paranoid network of police and government spies. Bill C-51 allows some 17 different government departments to share and create their own databases with this information and with other extremely personal information that the government currently holds, like our tax information. There is no possible way to guarantee the security of this information because there is no oversight, and it will be in too many unknown places.

And, when we were complaining about the billion dollar price tag on the Liberal gun registry, we would have fallen over in shock if we had been told that our own Conservative government would spend $4.2 billion dollars on a spy palace, complete with duck pond, for their secret police in the Communications Security Establishment.

So, the Conservative Party repealed the gun registry. Yes, they did. But, they replaced it with something far more sinister, with a far broader application.

During the Committee hearings for Bill C-51, many people begged the Harper government to amend the bill. They were given expert evaluations of the law and suggestions as to how to amend it so that it would accomplish its security goals while protecting the rights of innocent citizens.

I had an opportunity to make a brief statement at the committee hearing, but, given the quality of expert evidence that was being presented by people more qualified than me, I chose to appeal to the Conservative panel members who had voted to repeal Section 13. I told them that Bill C-51 was bad for all of the same reasons that Section 13 was bad, and I asked them to reconsider.

All of our pleas fell on deaf ears. A few days later, Conservative Committee member Diane Ablonczy famously used "air quotes" when she spoke of "rule of law". She said:

> Now the judge has to also consider ... something like 'rule of law', they have to consider things like 'principles of fundamental justice,' whatever *that* is ... There would be

such a morass of opinions and considerations that action would be pretty much at a stalemate.

As she said "rule of law", she made a contemptuous quote motion with both hands in the air like the movie character Dr. Evil. It was obvious the Conservatives wanted Bill C-51 to pass without any consideration of such a thing.

And, pass, it did.

All of the proposed amendments of the opposition were ignored and the Conservative Party used their majority to pass the worst piece of legislation this country has ever seen.

How can we claim to stand on our conservative principles if we remain silent in the face of such an attack on our fundamental rights? If we care about our country, should we not fight just as hard against unjust legislation that was drafted by our own guys as we did against the similar legislation that was drafted by the other guys? I suggest that we should fight even harder. And, I strongly believe that we need to make our opinions known in this election.

I have spoken to a lot of people about this election - a lot of conservatives. Many have expressed frustration, but many have said that they feel they have "no choice" but to vote for the Conservative Party because it is better than the alternatives.

I recently said that I wish I had a dime for every time a Conservative urged me to vote for my CPC candidate by saying that Stephen Harper is "the least of four evils". Really? Is that how we choose our leaders now?

But, the question is, is Harper really better than the alternatives? We know that the Harper government has fallen down on issues like Bill C-51 and lawful access. But, how are they doing in other areas?   Is it worth keeping Harper around because, despite his failings, he is upholding so many of our other conservative principles that it is in our interest to overlook his failings?

Below are some of the major areas of interest that many Canadian conservatives hold dear, along with my own short assessment as to how the Harper government is doing in each of those areas. You may not agree with all of my conclusions, but I think it will help to pinpoint the issues.

Social conservatism

If you are a social conservative, you were thrown under the bus before the Conservative Party ever came to power.   In fact, before the Conservative Party even existed.

Stephen Harper's campaign team made is clear when he was running in the election against Stockwell Day that they thought social conservatives were just a special interest group. Many of you knew that if Harper was elected it would be a fight to be heard from that point on. And, you were right.

One of the first things Stephen Harper did as the new leader of the Canadian Alliance was to take a hard-won and expensive nomination away from a prominent young social conservative, Ezra Levant, and insert himself into that riding.

The next thing he did is to start purging duly elected social conservatives from the party National Council.

At the first Conservative Party convention in Montreal he interfered in the policy amendment vote on partial birth abortion, misleading some of you into voting against it by promising you a parliamentary debate on same-sex marriage.

He then betrayed the people who took him at his word by merely having a vote on whether to debate same-sex marriage where, not surprisingly, Members of Parliament voted no.

No party leader has made it clearer that his government will never allow debate on the issue of abortion. He's been abundantly clear on this issue and there is no reason to think that after 9 years he is going to suddenly change his mind. This is especially obvious now that he is also refusing to address the issue of assisted suicide.

If you are a social conservative and you have a Conservative Party candidate who is socially conservative, you might, for good reasons, make a decision to vote for that person. But, it is beyond naive to think if your candidate wins and Harper is his/her leader, that your person will have any sway or any voice when it comes to social conservative issues.

If you are a social conservative voting for the Conservative Party, and your local candidate is not socially conservative, you might as well be voting for any other party on the ballot because the result will be the same. I would go as far as to say that if you are a social conservative and you keep voting for Stephen Harper, all you are doing is reinforcing his notion that he has to do absolutely nothing to retain your support. Meanwhile, you are contributing to the marginalization of so-cons within his party.

If social conservatives want to be heard in the Conservative Party, Stephen Harper must go. The only way for that to happen is for him to suffer an electoral defeat.

You can keep enabling him by propping him up and hoping that, despite nine years of history that shows otherwise, he will suddenly start respecting you. Or you can show him the door.

Economics

Many people voted for Stephen Harper because of his economic credentials. They felt that he had a strong grasp on those issues and that he could help keep Canada economically secure.

The economy is not the focus of this book, but even Maclean's magazine wrote an article in April of this year discussing Stephen Harper's economic record. It was entitled, "Stephen Harper: Conservative? Maybe not."

It is frustrating and disappointing to old Reformers, who successfully pressured the Liberal government to eliminate their serial deficits, to see that Conservative government turn those yearly Liberal surpluses back into deficits again.

It was beyond embarrassing during the first debate to see NDP leader Thomas Mulcair chastising our Conservative Prime Minister for running 8 deficits in a row!

Their millions of dollars of spending on advertising is a shameful waste of our tax money. As is their glut of pre-election spending in swing ridings, and the unprecedented extended writ period.

And, spending over a billion dollars on a "spy palace" for their CSEC agents is inexcusable. When are we going to start calling this most expensive government building ever built in Canada a "4 billion dollar boondoggle"?

Maybe you still think that Stephen Harper can do a better job handling the economy than the other party leaders. But, I submit to you that we have had better success moving the economy in the right direction when the other guys were in power and we were pushing them from the opposition benches.

I'm not crazy about the idea of the Liberals or the NDP handling our economy, but if they were doing as lousy a job as Stephen Harper is, we'd be getting off our collective butts and doing something about it instead of giving them a free pass.

Mulcair or Trudeau handling the economy with a strong an vocal opposition scares me less than Harper handling it unopposed by a neutered grassroots.

Guns

Gun owners have long been supporters of Stephen Harper because the Canadian Alliance promised to repeal the long gun registry. Although the Conservative Party has done that, it is important to keep in mind that, even if you are no longer in a long gun registry, under Bill C-51 you will be in any number of government databases, and your information can be shared with anyone. Are you really ahead of the game, or did you just get suckered in another Harper bait and switch?

And, what has happened to Bruce Montague and his family, under Conservative watch, is utterly shameful.

Stephen Harper has already been making the rounds trying to scare gun owners into voting for him because he says the Liberals would recreate the gun registry. It is important to look at what he has actually done and ask yourself if he is trustworthy on this issue.

Considering the privacy nightmare he has created with lawful access legislation and with Bill C-51, and considering the embarrassing amount of money he has poured into a "spy palace", how much do you trust him to not come back and create that "firearms control system" he said he was going to create to replace the long gun registry? If he did it, do you think it would respect your privacy or your property rights? Do you think it would be less expensive than the "billion dollar boondoggle", C-68? It is worth thinking about.

The National Firearms Association opposed Bill C-51 because they were very alive to its danger, and the High River gun grab happened under Harper's watch.

It would be a grave miscalculation for gun owners to assume that their best choice is Stephen Harper.

Terrorism

Some conservatives think that they need to vote for the Conservative Party because they will protect us from terrorists.

The truth of the matter is that Stephen Harper's government is cynically using global terrorism as an excuse to expand their surveillance and disruption programs against innocent citizens.

When ISIS releases their videos of them torturing and killing people in the most gruesome ways possible, they hope that people will spread their message far and wide. Many people, myself included, refuse to watch them or link to them or acknowledge them in any way. Helping the enemy spread their propaganda is inherently wrong.

The Harper government, on the other hand, decided to spread that propaganda further by setting it to music - the ISIS anthem - and inserting it into an election ad to promote themselves.

Even if you can get past the fact that they were propagating the very video ISIS wants to be spread, there are other very important principles that are violated when you use footage like that for your own purposes.

This is video of real innocent people in the final moments before their violent and horrific deaths. They did not consent to have that video taken, and they certainly didn't consent to have it shown to the world as a political ad for Stephen Harper. The fact that they would stoop so low as to use enemy propaganda in their campaign shows that they are totally out of their league when it comes to combating terrorism.

Much has been made about the attack on Parliament Hill by the lone terrorist shooter. It was a scary situation for sure, and incredibly sad for the family and friends of the brave soldier, Nathan Cirillo, who lost his life in that attack.

But, this incident has been used to try to scare Canadians into giving up our freedom and privacy in the name of security.

Although this is only peripherally related, I think that this incident gave us some insight into Prime Minister Harper's ability to lead in a crisis situation. It is understandable that the RCMP would want to protect the Prime Minister and that that would be their primary concern in an attack. That being said, the pictures of what was taking place inside the Conservative caucus room tell a sad story.

The pictures show that terrified Members of Parliament have piled all of the furniture up against the doors and they are trying to make spears out of flag poles so that they might have a chance of defending themselves if the shooter, or shooters, manage to make it into the room.

There is, of course, no sign of Stephen Harper because he was hiding in a broom closet. As he told Peter Mansbridge on CBC News later, "My first responsibility is to extricate myself from such a situation so I can continue the normal functions of government and obviously extraordinary functions on a day like that."

While it is clear that that is the security protocol the RCMP follows in these situations, I can't really imagine how an able-bodied man could follow a direction to take the only spot in the broom closet, leaving a quadriplegic man defenceless in the path of a madman.

I'm not sure what this new thing is with leaders hiding. I know that George Bush did it after 911, too.

But, in the old days, leaders did not cower in the face of danger. Often they were on the front lines. And I have to say that, without exception, every real conservative man I have ever met would have given that closet to Steven Fletcher and all of the women he could pack in there, and then went out to help the men make their spears. He had an opportunity to show that he was willing to stand up to terrorists and he, instead, showed he was afraid of them.

Bill C-51 is supposed to protect us from terrorism, but experts have shown that it not only violates the rights of private citizens, but it is ineffective and that it might even be detrimental to that goal.

Instead of listening carefully to the people with expertise and working to improve the bill, Stephen Harper and his government arrogantly dismissed all offers of advice and assistance and pushed through a defective bill that will, undoubtedly, be overturned by the Supreme Court of Canada.

This is not leadership on the issue of terrorism. It is incompetence. In these days of uncertainty, we need leaders who are willing to listen to security experts, not people who let their arrogance and inflexibility lead us into even more danger.

Foreign Policy

When it comes to foreign policy, Stephen Harper's support for Israel is something that I agree with. But, some of the decisions he has made in how to relate to the rest of the world are downright appalling.

Every Canadian knows that our northern border is completely undefended. The amount of money it would cost to equip and place our military in the north to protect it is completely untenable. Russia is on the other side of that border.

With complete disregard for the safety and security of Canadian citizens, Stephen Harper continually shakes his tiny fist at Russia's president Vladimir Putin, calling him an "Imperialist" and accusing him of threatening global peace and security.

He continues to add more sanctions and travel bans against Russia like he is the leader of some world super-power instead of the relatively unimpressive leader of a militarily weak country, repeatedly biting the ankle of a potentially dangerous and powerful adversary.

Conservatives understand that there is a time and a place for war. We are not unrealistic. But, Stephen Harper seems to be so determined to drag us into a war that we are unequipped to fight that we, as citizens, need to start questioning his motivation.

The reality is that it is our sons and daughters that will pay the price if Putin gets tired of Harper's yipping and decides to give him the fight for which he is spoiling.

Stephen Harper is the guy who literally hid behind a quadriplegic man when a lone gunman attacked the House of Commons. Do you trust him to bravely lead an under-equipped military into battle in our own country against one of the world's biggest military threats?

A true conservative does a risk/benefit analysis before they make a major decision. Attempting to drag our country into an avoidable military situation where the odds are stacked against us is not brave. It is irresponsible. And, it certainly isn't conservative.

Canada's hawkish new image has hurt our credibility on the world stage. We used to be seen as a peace-loving nation that would stand up to bullies, but would prefer to go out of our way to provide comfort and peacekeepers in war-torn countries.

Thanks to Stephen Harper we now look like America's "mini-me", foolishly pretending we have a Royal Flush when the whole world knows we are holding a pair of 10s.

Stephen Harper's foreign policy is not making us more secure, it is jeopardizing our security.

Grassroots Democracy

The Reform Party and the Canadian Alliance were based on principles of populism and bottom-up governance. One of the big selling points when the Liberals were still in power is that a Canadian Alliance (later Conservative Party) government would increase accountability and transparency, decrease the size of government, allow Members of Parliament to vote freely, and listen to the grassroots party members.

Unfortunately, the minute Stephen Harper became leader of the Canadian Alliance he started acting contrary to those principles. His disregard for the democratic choice of the riding association in taking Ezra Levant's nomination was step one. The dismantling of the freely-elected National Council was the next step, and, every time he had an opportunity to behave in a democratic fashion he instead concentrated power in his own office. Even his merger with the Progressive Conservative party was strongly opposed by the majority of the members of both parties.

It should be no surprise, then, that he shut down his Members of Parliament and began shutting down debate in the House of Commons. Because the party policy allowed Members of Parliament to vote freely on all bills that were not budget bills, he simply started making huge omnibus bills with budget measures and controversial legislation put together in the same package, thus allowing him to whip his MPs on nearly everything he considered important.

After promising Canadians and party members an elected Senate he, instead, stacked the Senate with his own cronies just like every other Prime Minister that we complained about in the past. When threatened with a confidence vote, he prorogued Parliament to avoid it.

Once he attained his majority government he became a one-man-show. Introduce a bill, throw some budget stuff in there, whip the caucus to get it through the House of Commons (and limit debate so you don't have to listen to objections), then get the Senate majority to pass it. Repeat at will.

No matter how much you want to support Stephen Harper, if you care about principles of democracy and transparency, you have to admit that things have never been this bad. And, even worse, he is paving the way for future Prime Ministers to act in a similar, dictatorial fashion when he eventually loses power.

Mr. Harper has repeatedly behaved in ways that we would not have tolerated from the Liberal Party. He continues to do it because he arrogantly believes that we have nowhere else to go. He thinks that if he just puts out enough attack ads making Justin Trudeau look bad, his own party members will fall into line and vote for him out of fear. So far, it has worked like a charm.

But when do we look at what he has done and admit to ourselves that this government looks nothing at all like what we envisioned a Conservative government to look like? When do we finally admit that the Emperor has no clothes? He calls himself a conservative, but he makes Brian Mulroney look like Ronald Reagan by comparison.

Look at the history. You can usually tell what a person will do in the future by looking at what they have done in the past. We have seen Stephen Harper in action since 2002 and he has shown less respect for our values than was shown by Jean Chrétien and Paul Martin. At least those two responded to our opposition pressure and did things like balance the budget! Stephen Harper has us on permanent "ignore", and party members are so afraid to rock that boat that they literally sit there and let him strip our rights in ways that no former Prime Minister would have ever dared. Brian Mulroney certainly went nowhere near as far and we all got up and left his party.

It's like Conservative Party members are suffering from collective post-traumatic stress disorder from the ordeal of leaving, starting a new party, and re-joining the Conservatives. Or, perhaps it is a kind of political Stockholm Syndrome and we have reached the point of actually identifying with the guy who literally kidnapped our party, removed the power from the grassroots and made it the Stephen Harper Show, then, every election, rubbed our noses in the fact that we had nowhere else to go.

Even now, as the election progresses, it has come to light that members of the public who attend Harper's campaign events are being forced to sign non-disclosure agreements! The most frightening part of that is that there are actually still people who are willing to do that for him!

Whatever it is, it is time we woke up and took our party back. Given what happened with Bill C-51, we have a responsibility as conservatives and as Canadians to withhold our votes from both the Conservative Party and the Liberal Party.

Maybe there will be enough of us to keep Harper from winning another majority and continuing his contemptuous Harper Show. Although that might help somewhat, it might only slow things down a little because Justin Trudeau has shown that he is quite willing to work with Stephen Harper to pass even the most egregious of legislation. But, perhaps we could work within the party framework and request a leadership review at that point. I am no longer a member of the CPC, but I would rejoin to help if there was a grassroots movement to get back to the basics.

If the previously unthinkable happened and the NDP formed our new government, that is not even something that I think we should fear. We have a history of strong performance in an opposition capacity and I believe we could do that again. If the worst happens, the NDP does a stint and it hurts our economy but they repeal Bill C-51, then we are still in a better position at the end than we were in the beginning. The economy can be fixed. The lives of people who have been "disrupted", spied on and ruined by unaccountable government agents cannot be as easily restored.

It's time for conservatives to find our collective backbone and clean house. A huge number of CPC Members of Parliament have already left so it is a great time to take back control and steer the conservative movement back on course.

Several people have asked me lately how I intend to vote. Because of the new riding boundaries, the Conservative candidate in my riding is Scott Reid. I have always had a great deal of respect for Scott. His commitment to democratic principles was stellar, and I would have walked to a polling station to cast a ballot for him.

Unfortunately, Scott Reid, like most of the Conservative MPs, voted for Bill C-51. Therefore I cannot, in good conscience, vote for him or his party. At this point there is no Libertarian candidate or any independents. I will not vote for the Liberal candidate for the same reason. So, that leaves me with a choice between the NDP and the Green Party.

I haven't decided for sure yet, but I am strongly leaning toward the Green Party. If I thought the NDP had a chance of winning this riding I honestly might choose to vote for them. But, I kind of like the idea of giving my vote to the Green Party because Elizabeth May, despite our obvious political differences, is the one leader who has consistently stood up in the House of Commons and fought for democracy, openness and accountability.

We all have to do our own analysis, but I hope we will all start by doing our duty as Canadians and holding Stephen Harper accountable for the direction he has gone. When you go to the polls in October, vote for a party that didn't vote for Bill C-51 and encourage all of your friends to do the same. No more enabling this sick kind of pseudo-conservatism. We deserve better than that, and so does Canada.

ABOUT THE AUTHOR

Connie Fournier is co-founder of the conservative internet forum, Free Dominion.

She has been politically active since 2001, running Free Dominion, sitting on the local Boards of Directors of both the Canadian Alliance and the Conservative Party of Canada, usually as Vice President.

She has organized rallies, petitions, banquets, fundraisers and other events in a volunteer capacity, and worked for a federal Member of Parliament for about two years.

In 2012, she was awarded the Queen's Diamond Jubilee Medal by federal Member of Parliament, Maurice Vellacott. He wrote:

Connie has been on the front lines of the battle to preserve fundamental freedoms in Canada...Through it all she has stood tall, and defended freedom for all Canadians.

Connie is happily married to her husband Mark and they have the most magnificent kids and grandkids in the whole world! :-)

INDEX